Palgrave Studies in Economic History

Series Editor
Kent Deng
London School of Economics
London, UK

"Landed estates and their owners have long dominated the political, social and economic control of the English countryside. In this masterly survey of their development since the mid-seventeenth century, Eric Jones uses a potent mix of well-chosen case examples and select economic concepts to draw out their character in a way that convincingly challenges past ideas about them.

His overarching thesis is that despite the changes of ownership wrought by otherwise disruptive socio-political events like the Restoration or Glorious Revolution, and despite their ranks having to absorb estate owners from wholly different backgrounds to those whose pedigrees had long been planted in the soil, including many deep-pocketed industrialists and successful mercantile families, the shared ethos and behaviour of those who possessed landed estates remained consistent in what they stood for and the self-referential values which they collectively projected.

Across chapters whose coverage ranges from how owners of such estates dealt with their tenants or those who dared to poach their game, to how they sought to exclude others from their private space and gaze both within their mansions as well as without, Jones highlights their persistent organisation around control, self-interest and leisurely indulgence. With his trademark interweave of well-researched case-studies and broader insightful observations and a willingness to challenge basic assumptions, Jones has produced a study of landed estates and their owners that—in the language of the chase—succeeds in flushing out from cover many new issues and debates that will surely run and run."
—Robert Dodgshon, *Aberystwith University, Wales*

"Eric Jones, one of the most respected and original economic historians of our age, has produced an indignant and sparkling indictment of landed estates in rural England. He mercilessly dissects the economic follies, environmental destruction, and social travesties committed by a callous gentry class in search of luxurious mansions, hunting grounds, and rustic views."
—Joel Mokyr, *Northwestern University, United States*

Palgrave Studies in Economic History is designed to illuminate and enrich our understanding of economies and economic phenomena of the past. The series covers a vast range of topics including financial history, labour history, development economics, commercialisation, urbanisation, industrialisation, modernisation, globalisation, and changes in world economic orders.

More information about this series at
http://www.palgrave.com/gp/series/14632

"Landed estates have been a defining feature of English society for centuries. In this book, Eric Jones provides us with a rare overview of their history as a single narrative from the mid-seventeenth century through to present times. His account is vivid, learned and elegant. It not only skilfully elucidates the malleability that underpinned the estates' survival through a procession of wars, depressions and major economic changes, but also examines aspects of their impact that have hitherto been typically less well explored in the literature, such as the estates' roles in the erosion of public rights of way, in the socially destructive remodelling of the landscape, and in the environmental harm wrought by blood sports. Viewed from this broader perspective, the landed estates of England are revealed more as sources of social stagnation and inequality than economic growth. Deeply researched and cogently argued, Jones' *Landed Estates and Rural Inequality* sheds important new light on the relationships between landownership, economy and society in English history."
—Gary Magee, *Monash University, Australia*

"Jones presents an overview of the English landed estate system from its medieval origins to the influx of industrial capital in the nineteenth century. He demonstrates that it was not only the concentration of capital in the landed class which defined and perpetuated social inequities, but also how the capital was deployed in re-shaping the countryside to service the leisure as well as the business interests of the land owners and their upwardly mobile tenants."
—Patrick Dillon, *University of Exeter, United Kingdom*

Eric L. Jones

Landed Estates and Rural Inequality in English History

From the Mid-Seventeenth Century to the Present

Eric L. Jones
La Trobe University
Melbourne, Australia

Palgrave Studies in Economic History
ISBN 978-3-319-74868-9   ISBN 978-3-319-74869-6   (eBook)
https://doi.org/10.1007/978-3-319-74869-6

Library of Congress Control Number: 2018934455

Cover illustration: Pattern adapted from an Indian cotton print produced in the 19th century

Printed on acid-free paper

This Palgrave Pivot imprint is published by the registered company Springer International Publishing AG part of Springer Nature
The registered company address is: Gewerbestrasse 11, 6330 Cham, Switzerland

For Michael Tarrant
Three-greats grandson of an Ashbury poacher

PROLOGUE

By the 1870s one-quarter of England was held in estates of over 10,000 acres and there were innumerable lesser ones. The existence and expansion of vast tracts of land in the hands of individual families brought with it a whole train of negative social and economic effects. Estates signalled enormous disparities in wealth and income, keeping ordinary citizens out of much of the countryside except as poorly paid employees, reducing the productivity of broad acres and hosting sports that abuse or kill wildlife. Positive effects, such as the agricultural improvements promoted by some landowners or the conservation of certain birds and mammals (in order to hunt them later), were real but seem of relatively minor consequence. Improvement and conservation could have been achieved by less exclusive and socially harmful means.

The historical analysis here starts in the mid-seventeenth century. Although estates had long existed, both the Cromwellian and Restoration regimes of the 1650s and 1660s decisively reaffirmed the existence of the landed system. What followed was a long-term increase in the number of estates, a growing privatisation of community assets and an enormous widening of the gap between social classes in the countryside. This book is an essay about these matters based on extensive reading, sometimes in minor sources, often very local ones. The narrative is built up from findings that are fungible, which is to say the examples cited are intended to stand in for others. There are too many fugitive references to list them all, which is not surprising given the existence of innumerable estates and villages, not to mention the even greater number of individual farm businesses. The material is to a large extent regional, although with a wider canvassing to confirm that the narrative and conclusions apply to lowland England as a whole.

The enclosure of common fields and suppression of rights over common grazing are well known but in this volume detailed attention is paid to the erosion of public rights of way, a process usually missing from historical writings. Special notice is accordingly taken of landscape effects, which are much downplayed by economic historians despite the considerable implications for capital investment as well as for social relations. These effects included building high walls that prevented the populace from enjoying the mere sight of parkland. More damagingly, a number of villages, even churches, were demolished. Engrossing or diverting public rights of way—road capture—was extremely common, as the assault on footpaths continues to be. These moves were the tip of an iceberg of landscape remodelling aimed at little of greater significance than securing privacy or improving the view from the big house. Amenity considerations like these are usually left to architectural and landscape historians who dwell on the aesthetic rewards and ignore social reality and economic implications. The highhandedness of estate building was mirrored by an often callous treatment of staff, indoors and out.

Still more explicit notice is paid in one chapter to the malign consequences for wildlife. A concern, not to say obsession, with blood sports was a major preoccupation of the landowning classes which has received less than appropriate notice in general histories or indeed modern studies. The almost universal organised cruelty towards animals, including birds and fish, takes some explaining. It represented status and occasion for male bonding. In this respect the text also rests on detailed local evidence. When the incidents are gathered together the cumulative impact of the abuse of animals, like that of social oppression, is seen to be devastating. These features of the English experience are easy to overlook given that the long period considered in this book also saw economic growth and industrialisation. Estate building typically involved the transfer of urban profits to the countryside and can be seen as an epiphenomenon of growth with significant collateral damage to the rural sector. This was not assuaged by the unintended consequence of providing a popular modern leisure resource in the form of country houses and parks belonging to the National Trust, membership of which approaches five million in the early twenty-first century.

Survival of the landed estate system through all the political and economic upheavals of time is a salient matter. The fact that agriculture was for so long the largest sector in the economy and was increasingly organised in the form of tenant farms on larger and larger estates guarantees this. Individual landowning families might rise or fall but the system itself persisted by continually regrouping. Those in power at the national level tended to be personally involved, took current arrangements for granted and made no great effort to abolish the order of things. The order prevailed despite the shift in emphasis within the farming industry brought about by the Repeal of the Corn Laws and the fact that spells of heavy taxation in the twentieth century may sometimes seem to have been threatening. Abiding support for the estate system was to be had because the land's amenity attractions and opportunities for social dominance repeatedly drew in new money. One chapter here deals with this topic in close-up—the inflow of cotton fortunes, mostly from Lancashire, into a single southern English region. This was an important episode in the investment in land of profits made elsewhere, a process that underpinned the persistence of the system as a whole whatever the misfortunes of particular families.

One aim of this book is therefore to counter the bland nature of so much literature on parks, estates and great houses—the roses which disguise the rural dunghill on which they were erected and on which the nostalgia and tourist industries rely. The celebration of these features tends to mention only *en passant*, if at all, the inequality inherent in the system and the social and environmental harm done. A majority of rural writing is adulatory rather than critical and at best neglects to highlight the costs of the long-prevailing inequality of land ownership. Even when the system's costs are introduced the relevant elements are fragmented and mentioned tangentially; here they are pulled together in approximately chronological order. Like many other English institutions, landed estates were neither designed for nor capable of producing economic growth or rural harmony. Far from it. Their role in agricultural production was only part of the story and not the main part. Estates increasingly became side effects of industrialisation and economic growth. This book demonstrates that the estate system was a drag on society and the economy rather than a boost. It tended to immobilise capital and enterprise in a landscape of pleasure for the few.

CONTENTS

CHAPTER 1

The Landed Interest

Abstract Ever since the Restoration of Charles II in 1660 the estate system imposed continuity on developments in rural society and on agriculture, which was for centuries the largest sector in the economy. The Glorious Revolution of 1688 was not the start of change but was a stage in the national expansion of commercial influence. The estate system was perpetuated by prolonged inflows of trading profits and the entry of new merchant personnel. They were absorbed sufficiently well for the landed interest to remain a cohesive elite which produced similar effects through time and space. Treatment of domestic servants was especially distasteful, including sexual harassment, and conditions were poor for farmworkers.

Keywords Domestic service • Estate system • Glorious Revolution • Investment of trading profits

After the Restoration of Charles II in 1660 the most powerful positions and profitable assets in the countryside were secured by the landowning establishment. Admittedly, sales of Royalist land during the preceding Interregnum had meant that part of the old gentry had been replaced by parliamentarians up to and including Oliver Cromwell, who received the Marquis of Worcester's estates. Yet under the restored monarchy a surprising number of the recipients succeeded in hanging on to their gains.

© The Author(s) 2018
E. L. Jones, *Landed Estates and Rural Inequality in English History*,
Palgrave Studies in Economic History,
https://doi.org/10.1007/978-3-319-74869-6_1

Charles II pursued men who had signed his father's death warrant but was otherwise inclined to let sleeping dogs lie. He did not wish to brew up another rebellion. Possession was nine-tenths of the law and the legal system certainly favoured landholders as a whole. In the next century their power facilitated the enclosures whereby the poor, even the second poor (those who kept themselves just above qualifying for poor relief), were often deprived of many rights. Despite even that consolidation of land in the hands of those who already owned a lot of it, scholars nevertheless see more continuity than change. Whatever happened to individuals, the prevailing organisation of landholding was disturbed but never overthrown.

The landowner class set about re-embracing the order it had been busily threatening in twenty years of military and political turmoil. It was good at reproducing itself. Unfortunate families might fall out of the system but the basic structure of rural society persisted through thick and thin. Changes in personnel there were but it seems hardly possible to compute how many. To make sure how much real alteration in family ownership took place, as opposed to changes in the standing of individual family members, each household would need to be examined—an almost unimaginably large task, certain to be frustrated by yawning gaps in the documents. Nor did the political changes, formative though some were, betoken epochal breaks of trend in the way land was managed—and that is the element which directly influenced agricultural productivity. Given agriculture's massive share in the economy, national economic security and growth rested on its productivity. Notwithstanding the appearances presented by a host of studies, rather little may be said about husbandry trends. The reason is that England is so very varied in geology and topography, and hence in ecology, that we do not know precisely how to sum up local research and offer a consistent account through time.

In the mid-seventeenth century upstart city lawyers and merchants displayed an urge to become respectable; the more corrupt their acquiring of estates had been, the greater the urge. Those who succeeded in camouflaging their moves merged back into the landed class and welcomed Charles II with one voice. Puritans sat in the first Restoration parliament and families in what might be called Team Puritan settled back into the unified ranks of landowners with remarkable ease. The Restoration was Animal Farm: like the pigs turning into the unlovely farmers of Orwell's book, the Puritans rejoined the ruling class despite its revamped Royalist air. When members of the older gentry who had been usurped during the Interregnum later bought their land back from its new Puritan owners, this placed a burden of debt on their estates, reducing the funds they had to invest. Royalists who completely sank under this burden during the Interregnum had been replaced but some Puritans were replaced in turn after the Restoration, in both cases by new 'improving' men, keen to recoup their own investments as well as raise their status. This helps to explain a measure of the agricultural advance in the middle decades of the seventeenth century. Agricultural development was already the watchword in Puritan times; at mid-century the successive editions of Walter Blith's *The English Improver Improved* were dedicated to Protector Cromwell. Under all regimes many members of the landed interest busied themselves with farming.

A challenge to the very idea of a landed interest, and of an identifiable national interest that it might influence, was mounted by Julian Hoppit. He located differences within the landowner class by examining legislation concerning estates, enclosures and land registries and implied that the landed interest was not as strong as it seemed because many parliamentary bills concerning these topics actually failed to pass into law. The parliament was not willing to push, say, for an overarching right to enclose; enclosures were proposed and tackled only one by one. But this is surely consistent with different assessments of specific prospects by individuals rather than the absence of a corps of landowners that had interests in common. Hoppit does make a number of distinctions among categories of landowner, noting points well known in agricultural history, for instance that the interests of proprietors in arable areas were prone to diverge from those whose holdings were primarily pastoral. For a very long time it was the arable sector, fronted by what the Victorians called the 'Voice of Norfolk,' that tended to dominate policy. Corn Laws designed to bolster profits from growing grain favoured arable farmers but simultaneously raised the cost of feedstuffs for livestock producers. Yet it was a long time before specialised regions fully supplanted mixed farming across the country and the agricultural interest accordingly retained a general similarity.

Splitting by locality and period can proceed almost indefinitely and nullify attempts to discern underlying patterns. Admittedly, few farms were exactly the same as others. They differed in location and market access, and possessed characteristics of soil and slope that affected management and productivity in ways not obvious from an overview. Estates may be thought of as 'bundles' of diverse units and were in their turn extremely varied. The great historian of landownership, John Habakkuk, no slouch at economic theory, found their diversity so extreme that he preferred to work empirically, moving from one example to the next. Yet social aspirations and pressures did lead to a basic convergence of behaviour to which new entrants soon conformed.

Even at the level of agrarian politics, Hoppit's case, which includes arguing that a unified landed interest could have existed only had there been a national agricultural policy for it to react against, carries splitting to extremes. Joan Johnson, in her close study of the Gloucestershire gentry, found the opposite, stating that for centuries the gentry formed, 'a united and socially compatible body'. As far as small farmers and village labourers were concerned, landed proprietors typically faced them with something of a common opposition, mobilising against their interests and against those of the consumers of bread as a whole. Underlings were in thrall to proprietors whose decisions were barely subject to sanctions and could be, to say the least, erratic: as Terry Eagleton wrote in the *London Review of Books* about a lunatic eighteenth-century member of the Wallop family, 'the line between eccentricity and insanity in the English aristocracy has always been hard to draw'. James Lees-Milne's *People and Places* gives the inside story, sometimes inadvertently, always revealingly, of relationships and behaviour among country house owners in the twentieth century. Such people felt free of ordinary constraints.

Distinctions did exist between 'landed interest' and 'estate system'. Sometimes they were subtle and sometimes marked. Hoppit's concern is with high politics and the currents of legislation rather than their direct impact on husbandry. He acknowledges that, despite internal differences that might reach down to disputes between individual owners, the landed interest as a whole was really quite powerful, achieving important and lasting legislation like the Game Laws that appealed to most of its members. The Game Laws permitted them to lord it over their poor neighbours in virtual perpetuity and it is with respect to this form of domination that the landed interest category is least to be doubted. The system was and is both resilient and elastic. Until 1870 it barely paused in growing, for all the political and economic hazards. Right up to the present, a fraction of the oldest landed families has retained a footing through every vicissitude, the most damaging being the great agricultural depressions, the loss of heirs in war and Lloyd George's taxes. While lesser operators fell at these fences, the great lords have constantly been joined by layer upon layer of men with new money. Seventy-nine mansions were demolished on the UK mainland between 1870 and 1919, years that were followed by a massive liquidation of estate acreage, but even today certain members of England's *ancien regime* survive on the land.

Possessing sufficient non-agricultural resources and being lucky about the lifespans of male heirs were requisites for the long-term survival of family estates, while selling off standing timber in emergencies was an expedient for those with inadequate liquid funds. One asset of an estate was woodland that could act as a bank deposit. Little could be done to guard against personal catastrophes or succour incompetents, but the attractions of estates guaranteed that the ranks of landowning families would be replenished, faster in times of national prosperity than was managed by the 'recession opportunists' who bought land in economic downturns, but nevertheless inexorably. Where one family fell, another rose—more and more as the economy grew. Any tightness in the land market meant business fortunes were spent on carving new estates out of former farmland.

This suggests a path-dependent thesis whereby landed society as a whole repeatedly renewed itself, not least via access to the political power which was shamelessly used to bolster the incomes and safeguard the wealth of landowners. The process may of course be made to seem smoother than it was by telescoping time as we look back; the record was mixed and not guaranteed to succeed in every case. In the generations and centuries after the Restoration there were still policy swings and external alarms but little resumption of the old interpersonal violence. Apart from Monmouth's Rebellion in 1685 and Judge Jeffrey's savage treatment of the prisoners, fatal affrays were rare in England. One of the last was in 1688 when Sir Richard Lovelace's men were attempting to join William of Orange and killed several of the Cirencester militia. But overall the stability described by J. H. Plumb in *The Growth of Political Stability in England* (1967) came to prevail. Violence was restricted to dealing with rioters and poachers and the dog-eat-dog conflicts among the landowners of the seventeenth century did not return. Energy was absorbed by elite politicking and naked force was deflected down the social scale.

Social divisions had been firmly in place long before the Civil War. They were gradually softening as the economy grew, increasing market activity and creating non-agricultural jobs. But from time to time efforts were made to turn the clock back. In the sixteenth century, the occasional pushy manorial lord attempted to assert that his tenants and everything they owned constituted his personal property; in short they were serfs. This retrogression was tried on ancestors of mine at Ashley, Hampshire, and represented an attempt at a shakedown in which the fictitious or archaic obligation could be bought off at a price. In the next century Charles I notoriously tried to revive feudal incidents. Like the Ashley landowner of Tudor times, he was trying to raise money. It did not work well in either case.

Calling these embryonic intentions feudal is misleading since feudalism implies mutual obligation between social levels. For the rich, such obligations were largely matters of choice and, if they were shouldered at all, were assumed in only minor ways—band aids, along the lines of a lady from the big house taking soup to sick cottagers. The hardening inequalities that continued through the Civil War and Interregnum and far beyond the Restoration were not so much features of winners and losers in a competitive market as of a harsh, highly regulated, economy. What were on the surface 'feudal' obligations, such as the requirement for tenants of the Leighs of Adlestrop to cart to the manor house one ton of coal from Tewkesbury or Evesham every year, were in reality contractual arrangements, rent in kind rather than an acknowledgement of social bonds. Any hope that the rich and powerful on either side during the Civil War seriously intended to reduce the underlying inequalities died when Cromwell stood the Levellers against the church wall in Burford and had them shot. Indeed, there are signs that inequality actually grew after the mid-seventeenth century: among the changes, average life expectancy and stature fell after 1650 despite economic growth overall, while from 1660 the experiment of writing documents in English rather than Latin was ended, and the squirearchy soon brought in laws restricting who could kill game.

The self-destructive violence of Civil War was afterwards replaced by parliamentary elections, and the polarity of religious strife gave way to the de facto agnosticism of eighteenth-century Anglicans, whose churches (as may readily be seen) flaunted the arms of earthly royalty. Intra-elite conflicts over resources and property, which in the early modern period had sometimes turned into brawls among armed retainers, were afterwards represented by squabbles over property bounds and enclosure, now fought by hiring lawyers and shuffling papers. Laxton, Nottinghamshire, was preserved as the classic survival of an open-field village by the prolonged squabble of two peers in the nineteenth century over the terms of enclosure. But landed society was not deeply concerned with who might prevail in such disputes. The precise membership of its own ranks was secondary to the interests of the whole. It was left to the individual to retain his or her position. Landed society was a system in aggregate whatever happened in detail.

The point is not advanced as acceptance that the property rights' regime instituted after the Glorious Revolution of 1688 was a legal rock on which a calmer society took its stance, much less that this was the ultimate spur to economic growth. It was not. Society muddled through without any organisational revolution. The Glorious Revolution is presented by influential historians and economists as having had immediate and perpetually beneficial effects through establishing secure property rights. The emphasis is almost entirely on the trustworthiness of the sovereign and the reliability of his or her commitment to keeping promises, not taxing subjects too much, paying off royal debts and so forth. It concentrates on high finance. The promises were important, but the greatest assurance that society desired of the monarch was that no king or queen would reintroduce the Roman Catholic faith. At the ground level, so to speak, a greater threat than royal chicanery was encroachment by one's neighbours, which is why dissension about boundaries was, as it continues to be, the prime source of legal disputes.

Even so, a leading school of thought, exemplified by Niall Ferguson's *The great degeneration* and Acemoglu and Robinson's *Why nations fail*, insists that 1688 established safe foundations for the market economy, and more than foundations, the engine of its propulsive power. It is not likely. Property rights were not drastically reformed under William III, disputes were endemic and persisted thereafter. Legal interests like the Law Lords continued for century after century to talk out proposals for a land registry that would have simplified transactions. The urgency with which the mantra of 1688 is pressed on developing economies today serves to mask the fact that growth in the exemplary case of England had more diffuse market sources. Chief among these was enough political security to encourage sufficient investment to overcome inadequacies in law and institutions. The degree of security need not be enormous; time and again we can sense that men tried to ignore national upsets and attend to their own business.

The proof of the pudding is in the eating: by 1688, commercial activity and economic growth had been evident for more than a generation. The Cromwellian period had not been one of stagnation; growth continued after the Restoration and went on through the Glorious Revolution. A paper by Steven Pincus and James Robinson catches this better; they propose that 1688 was not a unique, unheralded break but one of a series of changes that confirmed and rationalised an underlying shift in the balance of power towards mercantile interests and their representatives in parliament. Pre-existing growth was thus already altering England's political equilibrium in this direction. An important change was the fact that after 1688 economic policy came into the hands of party ministries rather than sets of personal advisers to the monarch such as the interlocking directorate which had created policy in the eight years following the Restoration of 1660. But that directorate, although accountable only to the monarch, had been a catalyst for expanding trade. Its members hoped to benefit themselves as much as King and country. In short, attributing growth and rising investment to the events of a given year, even 1688, or truncating the story by way of statistical series begun at that point, smacks of *post hoc ergo propter hoc*.

It is hard to believe that any single transition was responsible for growth, as if nothing was already happening. Such an approach credits the role of fragile political happenings, probably dependent on the agency of a few individuals, as being the source of what was in reality a broad cumulative process. Steering the process, as Charles II's directorate did, was not the same as initiating it. The approach is reminiscent of old sectoral explanations of the industrial revolution in which scholars put forward developments in one industry after another as the fundamental source of growth, on the dubious assumption that all other sectors remained quiescent until sparked by the one true cause. Cumulative growth begs for a less particular explanation, a path-dependent mechanism in which each sector, or the growth of each short period, led to the next. Trade expansion was a continuous, or at least a continual, spur. In the Pincus-Robinson view, this was what had shifted the balance of power into the hands of the modernising Whigs after 1688. All Whigs, though, were not merchants. The great Whig lords owned vast acres and were deeply involved in something less dynamic than trade—the estate system.

Histories of the very long term are open to the charge of over-generalisation, but are needed to sift the perpetual or recurrent from the transient or exceptional. The long view that follows in this and later chapters should not be taken as implying that all trends were linear, with no nuances, reverses or local exceptions. With hindsight we can see an underlying continuity from the 1650s or 1660s to the present day but it would overload the text to sketch every twist and turn. The central point is that landowners, once their factions were reunited in 1660, thereafter ceased to challenge one another in martial array. Although in later centuries the estate system was occasionally damaged by severe falls in the prices of farm products and was increasingly obliged to compete with rising urban and commercial interests, the arrangement was never again challenged by actual violence. It was the customary resting place for much of the nation's money, to which men retreated when parliament was out of session and to which families returned at the end of each London season. It established a hierarchy, accountable to no outsiders, and its interests, pastimes, style and manners never ceased to be the focus of emulation at home and abroad.

Those who bought estates remained on a pinnacle which others strove to reach. Estates were and to a degree remain the ultimate seducers of the English body politic.

The exodus of prosperous Londoners, of the rich from other cities like Bristol, and later of northern industrialists, lay at the heart of the society of rank that England persisted in elaborating. Their investment in land was the means of its perpetuation. The fluidity of English class relations is often contrasted with French and other continental rigidity. England's avoidance of revolution after the upheaval of Civil War is sometimes attributed to the (purely relative) ease of access to society's higher echelons. Agreed, not everyone among the *nouveaux riches* was drawn into an open landed class—open, that is to anyone with sufficient wealth. An urban bourgeoisie stayed content in London, while knots of the well-to-do tied themselves into the society of smaller towns, like the so-called Dawleish circle of former colonial administrators in Devon. Yet landed estates were the main story. They may be seen as central to reinforcing an ascriptive society often created in the first place by people who had, paradoxically, broken convention in order to rise up the social ladder by their own enterprise. Turning merchants, and later on manufacturers, into landowners whose descendants would accept leisured status as a birthright was a process that leached energy from commercial society. This may not have mattered much if blockages failed to prevent cohorts of fresh men rising by economic endeavour. Nevertheless, estates were machines perpetually dragging against change and causing resources to be sunk in rural gentility.

SOURCES AND FURTHER READING

Acemoglu, D., & Robinson, J. A. (2013). *Why nations fail.* London: Profile Books.

Blith, W. (1652). *The English improver improved.* London: John Wright.

Dick, O. L. (1962). *Aubrey's brief lives.* Harmondsworth: Penguin.

Eagleton, T. (2016, September). Review of Foyster, the trials of the King of Hampshire. *London Review of Books, 38*(17), 3–5.

Ferguson, N. (2014). *The great degeneration: How institutions decay and economies die.* London: Penguin.

Gilbert, K. (1992). *Life in a Hampshire village: The history of Ashley.* Winchester: Hampshire County Council.

Habakkuk, H. J. (1994). *Marriage, debt and the estates system: English landownership.* Oxford: Clarendon Press.

Hoppit, J. (1996). Patterns of parliamentary legislation, 1660–1800. *The Historical Journal, 39*(1), 109–131.

Hoppit, J. (2003). The landed interest and the national interest, 1660–1800. In J. Hoppit (Ed.), *Parliaments, nations and identities in Britain and Ireland, 1660–1850*. Manchester: Manchester University Press.

Jaeger, M. (1967). *Before Victoria*. Harmondsworth: Penguin.

Johnson, J. (1989). *The Gloucestershire gentry*. Gloucester: Alan Sutton.

Jones, E. L. (2013a). Gentry culture and the stifling of industry. *Journal of Socio-Economics, 47*, 185–192.

Jones, E. L. (2013b). Economics without history: Objections to the rights hypothesis. *Continuity & Change, 28*(3), 323–346.

Jones, E. L. (2017). *Small earthquake in Wiltshire: Seventeenth-century conflicts and their resolution*. Sutton Veny: Hobnob Press.

Keltner, D. (2016). *The power paradox: How we gain and lose influence*. London: Allen Lane.

Kenyon, J. (1988). *The civil wars of England*. London: Weidenfeld & Nicolson.

Lees-Milne, J. (1992). *People and places: Country house donors and the National Trust*. London: John Murray.

Nicolson, A. (2011). *The gentry: Stories of the English*. London: HarperPress.

Orwell, G. (1983). *Animal farm*. London: Penguin.

Pincus, S. C. A., & Robinson, J. A. (2011). *What really happened during the glorious revolution?* NBER Working Paper no. 17206, Cambridge, MA.

Plumb, J. H. (1977). *The growth of political stability in England 1675–1725*. London: Palgrave Macmillan.

CHAPTER 2

Cotton into Land

Abstract Land's attraction for outside capital was amplified by nineteenth-century industrial profits, helping to perpetuate and deepen the estate system. A concentrated study is made of Lancashire cotton masters as they entered land in sequence, first close to their mills, then further afield and finally in distant counties. Some chose to move to fashionable spa towns and all tended to furnish their houses with museum quality goods like paintings. Among receiving counties, Herefordshire and Gloucestershire, where money from the iron trade has earlier been deposited, are singled out. Entrants from the cotton industry successfully adopted the practices of elite landed society by becoming justices of the peace and deputy lieutenants of their adopted counties and by sending their sons to leading public schools.

Keywords Cotton industry • Gloucestershire • Herefordshire • Lancashire • Spa towns

Many fortunes made elsewhere were spent on buying country estates. During the early phases of industrialisation the investment involved mainly, but not exclusively, textile money, and within textiles money mainly, but not exclusively, from the cotton trade. This chapter will draw together

© The Author(s) 2018   11
E. L. Jones, *Landed Estates and Rural Inequality in English History*,
Palgrave Studies in Economic History,
https://doi.org/10.1007/978-3-319-74869-6_2

episodes in the use of profits from this source for buying land in a particular region on the western side of southern England. The approach illustrates the sequence of effects on agriculture and rural society and reduces the randomness that might come from cherry-picking examples all across the country. It also identifies links among participants.

Land was a magnet as the source of political power, social prestige and an enviable lifestyle, besides appearing to be a safe deposit for wealth. Buying land therefore reflected the three aims of status, consumption and investment, their relative proportions depending on circumstances and individuals. The habit goes back centuries. Although faltering at some periods, and despite precise motives fluctuating with circumstances, it has never ceased. The social and political 'necessity' of building up an estate was felt by many who acquired industrial fortunes during the eighteenth and nineteenth centuries. Such men, although seldom really from the wrong side of the tracks, as the mythology of rags to riches implies, were not as elevated socially as they or their wives and children would have wished. Their purpose was to establish themselves as what society considered to be high status. For instance, ambition for land overtook the Cropper family, paper manufacturers, who had achieved great influence around Kendal but considered that owning an estate would seal their position. They had business relations with the Crewdson and Horrocks cotton-spinning firm and were Quakers who turned Anglican. Quakers were conspicuous among early industrialists but joining the Church of England was a not uncommon feature of their social climbing, although the decision was usually taken by descendants rather than by the generation that first made big money. The Croppers' change of sect and purchase of land was a not untypical example of the course that new money took.

Parvenus might be disdained but for any of them with enough money it was eventually possible to acquire an estate and gain acceptance by the landed class. This qualified openness is held to explain the absence of political revolution in England. Allocating money from other sources to landed investments helped to reinforce and consolidate the stratum of the very rich who stereotypically passed much of the year in their rural mansions but spent the social season in the great town houses of London or (at earlier periods) in important county towns. This is not to say that every *arriviste* fortune was deposited in the countryside since a parallel London bourgeoisie also took root. Men of prestige (often military in origin) but with too little money or no desire to buy an agricultural estate were inclined to remain in provincial towns. But great accumulations of capital from court offices, the law, commerce and banking had long gone into estates in a great ring around London. Bristol's commercial cash was similarly invested, though on a smaller scale, and the vigorous springs of capital arising in the manufacturing districts were to follow suit.

Exactly what share of large urban fortunes entered the land in this way is a contentious matter that depends on how the statistical sources are interpreted and above all on what threshold definitions of wealth are adopted. At the opposite qualitative extreme there is much debate, not to mention selective quotation, concerning who was a gentleman, landed or not. Both approaches raise up their own difficulties, not made easier because the terminology of social status did not necessarily mean the same thing at every period or in every region and because the sources become thinner as one goes back in time. Notwithstanding these hesitations, there was clearly a considerable acquisition of estates by urban and industrial money over a vast area of England. The picture has often been painted with a broad brush. It raises questions concerning the land market, not all of which can be answered with available information but which nevertheless merit discussion. One issue relates to which industrialists chose to buy land and why and where. Newly rich industrialists had various options. They might stay put and plough their money back into the business, but for many of them, and especially for their offspring, the attractions of the mill wore thin after a time. Status, conspicuous consumption and more salubrious surroundings began to penetrate a successful manufacturer's mind, perhaps prompted by his wife and by a desire to elevate the next generation in society, even if the man were not socially ambitious on his own account.

Families at the very forefront of the industrial revolution certainly succumbed, if that is the right word, to the temptation of buying estates. Matthew Boulton's son and daughter-in-law, niece of the leading ironmaster, John Wilkinson, bought the village of Great Tew, Oxfordshire, which offers an instructive example of the costs and benefits of ownership through inheritance: the estate was reported as exceptionally well farmed in the 1870s whereas a century later the village itself was notoriously, even scandalously, tumbledown. Ironmasters as a whole had been quick off the mark with landed investment, the Knights establishing themselves at Downton Castle and the Foleys at Stoke Edith, both in Herefordshire. For the current exercise we can concentrate on purchases by cotton manufacturers, who became still more prominent among new entrants to land. With some overlaps, their purchases were first made within Lancashire, then sometimes further afield in the north and finally in the south of England, primarily in Gloucestershire and Herefordshire. In these counties there seems to have been a concentration of activity, although in the absence of full information about others this can be only a provisional view.

We possess only what might be called a haphazard sample of those who spent heavily on consumption, including estates, and it is not big enough to delineate phases of manufacturers' behaviour categorically. Courses of action altered over time even within the same family. It might be that sending sons away to expensive schools indicated social ambition and was a forerunner of big outlays on physical forms of consumption; this suggestion would be testable in principle, though vulnerable to small sample size. The most obvious initial purchases by the cotton masters were houses and land not too far away from the mill. Other locations, by no means incompatible with the first, were second homes in the more attractive parts of Lancashire: Lytham St Anne's comes to mind. Purchasing complete estates followed, the early ones still being in the vicinity of the industrial areas. Simultaneously, or alternatively, some manufacturers spent heavily on furnishings and paintings for the house and occasionally on building major collections of what were, or later became, museum exhibits. Blackburn and other museums have been major beneficiaries, some of them outclassing London in scale and quality of holdings. In recent times a 'Cotton into Gold' exhibition (ironically staged in London) celebrated the fact.

Objets d'art had a potential resale value, yet produced no income. On the other hand an estate was expected to contribute an annual return from farm rents. Consumption and lifestyle might continue to be the main attraction but the cotton masters could see that landed families did profit financially from their broad acres—more than one generation of the Townleys of Burnley, for instance, built up the family's estates in order to generate even more income than they already had. Tastes differ even within the same family: when Peregrine Townley rebuilt Townley Hall he sold his father's excellent book collection to pay for it and later went on to buy more land for the sake of the rental income. Levels of profitability in the landed sector are obscured by the fact that, as a result of large sums being lavished on landscaping and ornamenting the big house, returns to an estate were likely to fall short of what farm rents could cover. Generally speaking, the rate of return on land was acknowledged to be lower than from other investments, besides the relative illiquidity of the asset.

We may surmise, but cannot prove, that the expectations of incomers about financial returns from land were over-optimistic. Such a hope might be encouraged by observing that the landed class lived comfortably, even luxuriously, without seeming to make much personal effort. Manufacturers might therefore assume they could manage the business of an estate better than such lackadaisical incumbents. Further encouragement might come from the fact that many purchases took place during the last quarter of the nineteenth century when land prices had fallen in the arable depression, meaning that less capital would have to be risked than during the preceding 'Golden Age'.

Purchases of Herefordshire estates by Lancastrian industrial money began as early as 1799 when William Higginson bought Saltmarshe, Bromyard, and continued into the twentieth century, with a peak during the third quarter of the nineteenth century. Nothing was really new about textile money entering land in western and central southern England: Gloucestershire, once partly industrial, was noted for the eighteenth-century buying of estates by woollen manufacturers from the Stroud valley. They were the 'Gentlemen Clothiers' and theirs was a mini-migration within their home county, just as the great nineteenth-century producers of cotton were to dip their toes first in their own county of Lancashire. Earlier still Thomas Dolman, king of the spinners of wool in Newbury, had come to Gloucestershire from Berkshire in 1558 to buy Winchcombe Abbey Manor and in 1571 to acquire Stanton, an estate he bequeathed to his son, Mathias. Thomas had already built Shaw House at Newbury for himself, become a country gentleman and abandoned the spinning trade, hence the Berkshire lament, 'Lord have mercy upon us, miserable sinners, Thomas Dolman has built a new house, and turned away all his spinners.'

Whatever Thomas's wishes for the advancement of his family, his son became and remained a haberdasher and citizen of the City of London. He did not found a landed dynasty in Gloucestershire, instead selling off Stanton in lots to the copyholders. Hence this particular transfer of industrial capital to the land might be said to have gone off half-cock or at least to have been a poor predictor of what was to come. The Gentlemen Clothiers were better guides. They desired a rural life, provided they could retain oversight of their businesses. Rich they may have been but typically they stayed too close to their mills to disguise their origins. Great wealth was enough to differentiate them from their employees and other inhabitants, leading an American author to imply that the gap mirrored that between planter and slave. This is surely an exaggeration but on the other hand English authors, accustomed to steep hierarchy, may take wide social distance for granted and minimise the gap.

The continued proximity of the Gentlemen Clothiers to the mills meant that the first generation to acquire estates did not break with industry in the way Thomas Dolman had done. But as with every aspect of landed investment there were exceptions and Gloucestershire woollen clothiers were still buying estates when the cotton magnates were only just beginning to do so. Charles Ballinger, from Chalford, was described as the son of a rich woollen clothier and as being a rich clothier himself, as well as a rich landowner. He built Skaiteshill House at Chalford in 1805 but about 1810 moved right away to construct Glewstone Court, Goodrich, Herefordshire, becoming a justice of the peace (JP) and prominent personage in that county.

What happened when the industrialisation of the north of England created a new stream of entrants was different again, not that investing industrial profits in land was novel within Lancashire. Discreet investment had a long run in both directions and the small size of the cotton towns meant that the countryside was always at hand. Leading cotton lords were members of the Manchester Society of Agriculture, the mere existence of which reveals that industrialists did not stay isolated from the farming world. A jump in the scale of land purchases took place at the end of the eighteenth century when textile production became very profitable. Cotton proprietors moved their residences somewhat away from the mills that were the sources of their wealth; a dispersal to distant counties followed.

The majority of big cotton spinners came from backgrounds that could provide support and capital from the start. Even so, the early cotton fortunes were often spectacular and obtained quickly, before further entrants to industry could increase competition and reduce returns. What to do with the extra cash? Just as individual desires determined how much was diverted into buying luxuries, personal interest determined what forms luxurious expenditure might take. Enough profit accrued to men who cannot have started life expecting to become super-rich hint that there were cases where the diminishing marginal utility of real income set in, prompting lavish or even trivial purchases. Paintings and more particularly *objets d'art* were not primarily investments but status symbols. They may have offered capital appreciation, as the purchasers doubtless understood, but this was surely not in the forefront of their minds. In their own county they could follow the precedent of great landowner-collectors such as Charles Townley (1737–1805) of Townley Hall, Burnley, who had made three Grand Tours and amassed an outstanding art collection.

The philanthropy that funded or subsidised art galleries, museums and churches might be a cause for approbation—there were worse outlets—but represented the private disposal of grossly unequal wealth and income.

Cotton hands, meanwhile, lived in back-to-back houses and worked long hours for low pay; their suffering in trade downturns is well known. The website of the church of St John the Evangelist in Knaresborough, North Yorkshire, a church which had been paid for by the cotton manufacturer, William Atkinson, is ungracious enough to point out this discrepancy and undoubtedly there was justice in the complaint. The expenditure on landed estates to which Lancashire cotton contributed prompted a surprising outburst from none other than Winston Churchill, who was appalled by the condition of the poor in Manchester. He visited Germany in 1909 and noted a positively un-English lack of walls around the great estates: 'All this picture', he wrote, 'makes one feel what a dreadful blight and burden our poor people have to put up with—with parks and palaces of country families almost touching one another and smothering the village and the industry'.

The sequence and scale of outlays by the cotton lords are hard to fit into a firm chronology because there were overlaps, besides different targets of expenditure that were not necessarily mutually exclusive. It is certainly not surprising that many of the earliest purchases of dwellings and property were not far distant from the sources of the money that made them affordable. John Horrocks, who was producing cotton from 1791, built Penwortham Hall just across the Ribble from Preston in 1801. His status was sealed the next year when he became a member of parliament (MP). Horrocks's firm continued in various combinations with other firms and was run by Thomas Miller from 1852. He exemplifies the difference that swelling wealth made with respect to the size of land purchases and large-scale art collection. Miller established his country retreat further away towards Blackpool by developing Singleton Hall and the villages of Singleton and Thistleton. He also bought 4000 acres in the Fylde, and built up a fine art collection. Singleton is only about fifteen miles from Preston, so the migration was hardly remarkable. During the 1850s Miller played the autocrat and supposedly pushed Roman Catholics out of his parish. After he died in 1865 his son, Thomas Horrocks Miller, built a mansion at Singleton and acquired the nearby Avenham estate.

Manufacturers were likewise moving out from Blackburn. In the 1890s they were building detached houses outside the town. They wished to escape the urban area but did not always hanker for huge rural or perhaps one should say agricultural properties. For much of the nineteenth century cotton in all its forms was profitable and those who prospered as a result, wherever they were and in whatever stage of the trade and industry they engaged, spent their money on conspicuous consumption. The numerous people in England who owned cotton-picking slaves, and whose names have been exposed by a recent University of London study, tended to live in stylish places. The large plantation owners of the Confederate states built ornate mansions. Almost all the cotton picked in Texas was shipped out of Galveston, whose business leaders built extravagantly ornate town houses with the proceeds.

At Blackburn an exception to the non-agricultural rule was Henry Ward, cotton manufacturer, who bought Salesbury Hall and rebuilt a number of seventeenth-century farmhouses on the manor. Growing towns nevertheless had a habit of catching up with those who moved out if they did not move far enough. The vicinity of Lovely Hall, Salesbury, north-east of Blackburn—a house owned by cotton masters at various periods and still advertised in 2015 as a 'dream property'—came to be surrounded by a network of footpaths. The paths were created by workers out for recreational walks, the opposite of the usual English story in which rights of way have been progressively privatised. Coal-bearing areas meanwhile were becoming so disturbed by miners who poached the owners' pheasants that they were vacated. Some properties were abandoned in favour of moorland estates, explicitly advertised as situated in zones of low population.

The purchase of estates was no limited phenomenon, though it is not immediately clear what proportion of the industrial rich might have been expected to participate. In his *Social History of Lancashire* Walton notes that estates had been bought by successful linen drapers well ahead of the cotton boom. As for purchasers from the cotton industry, he remarks that more work on out-movement needs to be done but does not comment further, perhaps understandably in that he is concerned with the county of his title and not with distant places to which rich Lancastrians moved. He does however report Howe's valuable study in *The Cotton Masters* concerning 351 textile masters between 1830 and 1860. Of these 39 or their direct descendants came to own estates of over 1000 acres in the Midlands or South and many others acquired smaller estates. Movement was particularly evident towards the end of the nineteenth century, when, as we noted, land prices had fallen. Howe's data show that in 1886 9.3 per cent and by 1903 11 per cent of Lancashire's county magistrates gave addresses outside Lancashire and the adjoining counties. This is suggestive, though it undoubtedly undercounts the scale of the exodus as a whole.

Many of the retreats were 'only' town houses rather than agricultural properties. The diaspora was wide. Leamington Spa was a favoured resort, as was Hove. Cheltenham Spa was another favourite; for instance, it was where Johan Frerichs, a Manchester cotton manufacturer originally from Bremen, built Thirlestaine Hall in the 1850s. A Yorkshire woollen merchant and manufacturer, John Dearman Birstall, bought Bowden Hall outside Gloucester, only a few miles from Cheltenham, in 1868 and developed a landscape garden. Cheltenham was especially popular with the second and third generations of textile families, such as John Frederick Lees, the grandson of an early cotton manufacturer and a mill owner himself. He was an Oxford graduate, MP for Oldham and is among the cotton men buried in Cheltenham. As a resort town Cheltenham was highly attractive to upwardly mobile mill owners; besides great town houses they bought land in the immediately adjacent countryside. About 1858 the Lancashire cotton manufacturer, William Hall, built Seven Springs House only four miles from the centre of Cheltenham and in 1878 his daughter built Ullenwood, a similar distance away. Both properties had some land. Five years later a retired cotton manufacturer, James Taylor, bought the Rendcomb estate of 4775 acres not many miles away.

Tim Procter comments that business historians have neglected the sons of the first generation except when they were young and at odds with their fathers. If the sons have been ignored, the daughters are even more difficult to trace since they are typically disguised under the names of their husbands and would require an extensive genealogical search to identify. Even when the women are found to have ended up as ladies of the manor in distant counties, it is hard to be certain whose money had been used to secure the position. This shows how tricky it is to decide where the profits from cotton as a whole went, given the geographical dispersal of industrial fortunes, the several ends on which money might be spent, and the big bequests left by businessmen and lawyers who were not primarily engaged in manufacturing cotton (though obviously beneficiaries of Lancashire's all-round prosperity). Only a very occasional note appears about the distaff side, as when we find that two daughters of George Walmsley of Peel Mill, Burnley, were educated at Cheltenham Ladies College. Their elder sister, who died in 1945, was a big donor to the art collection at Lytham St Anne's.

The flow of capital from industry into land was very considerable. It was the equivalent of so a large a proportion of the funds invested in manufacturing as to prompt the question whether the withdrawal was harmful to industry, even to the economy at large. Might early stages in the rate of growth have been faster had all profits been reinvested in manufacturing? (It is beyond contest that there would have been *social* gains, had provision for the workers, their housing and so forth, been more generous). Did it matter if the rewards of entrepreneurship were dissipated, as some might see it, on the adornment of distant estates and grand houses or the amassing of baubles that ended up in museums and galleries? The generations who followed each first thrusting businessman to make his pile did not engage so energetically in manufacturing; they were increasingly prone to gentrifying and to spending money. This is not unlike the Buddenbrooks thesis of economics textbooks, named after a novel by Thomas Mann, and referred to in Lancashire as 'clogs to clogs in three generations'.

Detachment from industry ended at worst in shabby gentility, which may have been a pose; in any case most descendants fared better than that. Measuring the success of succeeding generations in terms of accumulated or retained material goods implies a value judgement. A life of comparative ease or (say) artistic creativity may have been preferred over the effort needed to manage fortunes or properties. Nor, viewed from the standpoint of the whole economy, does there seem to have been a significant problem. It would have become one had there been insurmountable blockages to would-be new entrants once the first entrepreneurs had left. This was not the case in Lancashire. There were plenty of eager replacements.

Aspirants to the estate life there certainly were but the precise period when they moved made a difference to how satisfactory and enjoyable they would find the landowning or rentier life. Understandably, individual families faced a number of threats, such as failure to produce a male heir or the perverse achievement of spawning dilettantes or wastrels. It is possible to argue, as suggested above, that for one's offspring to be able to afford a life of genteel leisure, disguised perhaps by a little public service as a magistrate, was the ultimate purpose of buying into landed society. For them brazenly to waste one's money was altogether different. A prime case was that of the Peels. The father of Robert Peel, the prime minister, came from a Lancashire calico-making family—they had switched from the woollen industry. He bought an estate near Tamworth, Staffordshire, introduced cotton manufacturing there and built Drayton Manor. He can have had no doubts about the energy and worth of his politician son yet his grandson, another Robert Peel, was not merely a disappointment but a catastrophe. He gambled so heavily on horse racing that he had to sell much of the Drayton estate, including the manor. This was however scarcely typical; the commoner trajectory was in the direction of a routine landowning life showing little of the spark that had animated the founder of the family firm. Admittedly some were energetic and made a difference in their localities. Francis Cross (born in Bolton) was one of these, using cotton money to buy Aston Tirrold Manor, Berkshire (now Oxfordshire), becoming a JP and rejuvenating his property's distressed agriculture. But few if any found in farming a key to riches that paralleled the industrial achievements of their forebears.

Commercially there were two dangers: overconsumption of unproductive assets and miscalculation about future markets for farm produce. The lifestyle of a landed proprietor positively encourages extravagance, so a leading banker who had married into land observed to me. Investing in what turns out to be scarcely profitable enterprises on the farms may be a dead loss. Building or enlarging the residence and landscaping the grounds eat up money. The newcomers tended to hire expensive architects and interior designers and actively collected furniture and paintings, besides commissioning pictures of their mansion and estate. Spas were patronised and luxurious food and drink brought down from London purveyors. The aim was not to fit into rural society as a whole but to assimilate to the established county rich, who socialised and married within its own ranks. Industrial money entering land sometimes ruffled but never overturned existing social *mores*; the desire for acceptance led newcomers to mimic and reinforce the unequal arrangements of the estate system.

By strong inference, therefore, social acceptance was a major motive for the types of expenditure in which entrants commonly indulged, for example going at once to the educational apex by sending their firstborn sons to Eton or Harrow and putting them through Cambridge. This manoeuvre was obviously successful, as can be seen from the number of arrivals who became JPs and deputy lieutenants (DLs) or whose sons scaled these heights while at the same time marrying into the gentry or even the aristocracy. Richard Arkwright at Hampton Court, Herefordshire, one of the great cotton spinner's sons, had no immediate difficulty in being accepted. The Dukes of Rutland and Devonshire had been unwelcoming in Derbyshire but once he possessed an estate in Herefordshire the Duke of Norfolk quickly wrote with an invitation to dine and the offer of a few does to replenish the deer park.

Less gracious members of the rural establishment fought, as it were, rearguard actions. The crusty old banker, John Biddulph from Ledbury, cast a jaundiced eye around a dinner table and depicted most of his fellow guests as parvenus. Rev. Francis Witts dismissed Thomas Phillips, the great book collector of Buckland and Broadway, and his wife, as people who could make no claim to gentility, Phillips being the illegitimate son of a man who had made his fortune in the days when—Witts averred—easy money could be made by manufacturing cotton. Witts was a member of a particularly snobbish family, his aunt, Lady Lytellton, having gone so far as to found a spinning school at Malvern to check the evil of female servants dressing above their station.

One old-guard Herefordshire landowner even carped that Richard Arkwright, said by some to be the richest commoner in Europe, was a 'tradesman'. (Assertions that an individual was the richest in a whole society are not uncommon, e.g. Robert Stayner Holford [1808–1892] of Westonbirt, Gloucestershire, was 'supposedly the richest commoner in England', an accolade likewise bestowed on Arkwright and the rather later James Morrison, but such claims are not accompanied by documentation or calculations. They mean little more than that the individual was very, very rich). The remark about Arkwright was made when Richard's son, John, a Cambridge graduate, had already been High Sheriff of Herefordshire for two years. John ran the Hampton Court estate and his brothers were settled on large estates elsewhere in the country, one of them becoming sufficiently established at Mark Hall, Essex, to supply the model for Trollope's hunting parson.

The 'tradesman' remark was made in a submission to the Select Committee on Agriculture of 1833 by J. B. Turner of Brockmanton Hall, Leominster, who owned many other farms in Herefordshire and was active in promoting agricultural improvement, not to mention the establishment of a railway. Whence the animus towards Arkwright? Turner declared a background 'in trade' himself, having manufactured carpet in four places, indeed in a letter to the *Hereford Journal* (27/11/1844) he described himself as 'manufacturer, merchant and tradesman' besides 'country gentleman and farmer'. He left bequests to two nephews who were Manchester cotton manufacturers, apparently from the prominent spinning family of Guest, thereby revealing an unexpected link between Herefordshire farming and Lancashire industry. Turner's remark may not have been social snobbery like that displayed by Biddulph or Witts but political in origin. In 1847 he attended a dinner to celebrate the election as MP for Evesham of Captain George Rushout, who was listed among the members for Worcestershire as 'Protectionist'. Turner himself had been one of the founders of a farmers' defence society and in 1850 of an Association for the Protection of British Industry. The fact that the Arkwright family favoured free trade may have been what riled him.

At any rate the sourpusses did not prevail. One measure of the extent of assimilation is demonstrated by the descendants of John Wood, cotton spinner of Glossop, Derbyshire, fourteen miles south-east of Manchester. He owned the largest textile mill site in north-west Derbyshire and his family came to possess a London house, a big place in Suffolk and property in Herefordshire. A series of gentry and even aristocratic marriages by the sons and daughters of later generations create a genealogical tangle for the outsider. Suffice it to say that John Wood's only son was educated at Eton and married into the Bateman-Hanbury family of Shobdon, Herefordshire. He was a DL in both Derbyshire and Herefordshire, was elected an MP and eventually became a baronet. Similar achievements followed for others among Wood's descendants, one of whom (Rugby and Magdalen) was a Derbyshire MP, a Herefordshire JP and DL, and to crown his symbolic achievements, High Sheriff of Herefordshire. All this took place at the turn of the nineteenth and twentieth centuries and derived from cotton money.

Social climbing continued despite those who sneered. How long rising socially 'ought' to have taken is another somewhat moot question. Looking back we tend to telescope time but, given the rigid class conventions of the nineteenth century, the industrialists were surely both quick and successful at camouflaging themselves, or their children, with rural gentility. What mattered was education, conduct and visible opulence, as even John Biddulph acknowledged. Money talks if it hoists the right social symbols and new neighbours included some who were glad of loans from the incomers or of advantageous marriages with their offspring. Eton or Harrow and Cambridge were investments good at papering over the workaday beginnings of father or grandfather. Younger sons and later generations managed well enough even with lesser schools like Rugby.

As we have seen, the houses of the next tier of aspirants, those who lived genteelly but did not buy landed estates, tended to be in fashionable places: in Lancashire in Lytham St Anne's or at a pinch Southport, and away from the county in Leamington Spa, Cheltenham Spa or Hove. When John Arkwright was in poor health at mid-century he decamped from Hampton Court to Dover. The gravel heaths near Southampton were mentioned as another desirable location. An Arkwright descendant, Francis, lost a parliamentary election, went to New Zealand and built a house there but subsequently returned to Bournemouth. A mild climate was a draw, given unhappiness with (for instance) the cold Cotswolds, though life in salubrious south-coast patches of large villas was not attractive enough to divert the largest fortunes away from building up landed estates. Society was another factor in choice of location: the 'Season' may have helped to assuage rural isolation but we know that the wives of some people who owned estates found the countryside dull and hankered for smart company. Husbands had more outlets in the form of public offices and especially blood sports but the wives might prefer the spa, the villa or the coast.

Assimilation meant conforming to the *mores* of the landed rich. Because the new incomers were already rich and had been powerful in their workplaces, the exercise of dominance would not have repelled them. All they had to learn were the tribal ways and sense of entitlement of the landed class, which—at least for their sons schooled at Eton or Harrow—cannot have been challenging. It would have been congenial to lord it over a captive village population in the expected stylised manner: as Dacher Keltner has shown by observation and experiment in *The Power Paradox*, dominance behaviour is inherent in becoming rich. It comes with the territory. As Henry Adams said, 'power is a sort of tumor that ends by killing the victim's sympathies', an observation borne out by the behaviour of the landed classes to those they thought of as social inferiors. Whether incomers became, as it were, more royalist than the king is uncertain but not improbable.

A more benign aspect of assimilation was charitable work, though it seldom amounted to much more than choosing to recycle a tiny percentage of a family's wealth. Cottages were rebuilt more solidly than before, though never grandly, less being spent on them than on long park walls and other accoutrements of landed property. Examples of charity of the soup kitchen variety are legion, involving *de haut en bas* descents by the lord of the manor's daughters on the homes of poor villagers. The assumption was that behaviour of this type was right and proper. Presumably some visits were made out of genuine kindness, as when the spinster descendant of a family called Jones that had made its money out of house letting went to work in the London slums and thereafter lived a life of caring. Her money had derived from the rents of Lancashire back-to-backs, on the basis of which her grandfather had bought a Gloucestershire Manor in about 1895 and become a JP and DL, while her father too lived the life of a country gentleman. The choice of giving was arbitrary or personal rather than needs-based, and involved social engineering through being targeted at the so-called deserving poor. Talking to people who remembered these things one finds resentment as well as gratitude, especially among the menfolk. Help was usually directed at villagers on the estate, not at people around the works where the money was made, as when a rich Durham mining family set up a trust to provide the poor with coal at Botley, Hampshire (on William Cobbett's old estate!). The trust was still operating in the 1990s.

Along the continuum of movement from industry to land some men did take industry with them into the countryside, though this was rare. Most wished to escape the taint and smoke. Robert Peel, senior, we have noticed, introduced cotton manufacturing to Tamworth. From 1867 Joseph Jones, a mill owner of Oldham with additional interests in coal and banking, bought four Worcestershire estates totalling 8050 acres. Some of his land lay along what might be called the southern edge of industrial England. Together with the farmland, his family gained control of several coal mines at Abberley and Pensax which were working in a small way as late as 1935. Some of the Joneses' Worcestershire estates stayed in family hands until 1939 and it may be thought illustrative of the life course of such a family that a modern descendant is neither an industrialist nor a landed proprietor but an antique dealer.

Financial returns to the farming of estates were not outstanding and were vulnerable to downturns in product prices. Viewed with hindsight, the turnover of estates seems high. Related questions concern who sold to incoming industrialists in the first place and was there a pattern to this? As with the elusive fate of the farmers who left arable England during depression times, it is an obscure topic, requiring an intimate knowledge of recondite genealogies. Most of the research done on incoming farmers between the wars dealt understandably enough with men from Scotland and the West Country, who were highly visible when groups of them arrived to rent or buy farms. Those they replaced because they had failed were not thought to be especially interesting. It is rare to find any general statement about them, although J. B. Turner of Brockmanton Hall told the Select Committee on Agriculture in 1833 that those who had quit during the post-Napoleonic depression took up any sort of occupation they could get, becoming farm bailiffs, schoolmasters or clerks. Some may have fallen on the parish or obtained help from charitable friends. We may guess that others emigrated, taking themselves out of reach of local research. The replacement of landowners is a comparable problem: the incomers can be identified but who sold to them and why they did so are hard to discover and what happened to them and the purchase price is not easy to tell.

The experiences of the new owners of estates and their families changed according to two timescales: first, the stage in a man's life or the ages of his children at the date of purchase and secondly according to fluctuations in the larger economy. Within the general framework of upper-class behaviour, the heirs, who almost always were firstborn sons, might be chips off the old block but a fraction of the grandsons were undoubtedly less reliable. When large estates were bought it was in any case usual to leave day-to-day management to agents. The cotton lords were busy men and while confident of their own managerial prowess probably soon admitted to themselves they were out of their depth in the countryside. Their influence was channelled through professional agents who lacked the means or enterprise to farm on their own account but were happy to run an estate without risking such capital as they did have, while basking in the delegated power of rich employers.

The richer of the new owners, those acquiring extensive agricultural land, often set about remodelling their estates, especially if they were entering at times of farming prosperity. Their activity was likely to include rebuilding farmhouses and bringing farmsteads up to date, and might mean establishing entirely new ring-fenced farms. Looking around the modern landscape it is not hard to spot districts where the farmhouses still look alike, having been erected by some well-heeled owner in a few years of Victoria's reign. Like those of other landowners, the houses may sport the proprietor's initials and insignia and give the date of construction. How far investment by new owners cushioned local agriculture against falling commodity prices is unclear. Richard Arkwright's approach was ambivalent or rather variable. His son was more generous and, being conscious that he was a tenant himself, more inclined to believe farmers' protestations of hard times. Whether incoming owners in general behaved differently from the more energetic incumbents would require a matching study that does not appear to have been carried out. In some cases an incoming landlord was energetic enough to put arable farming on a successful footing, while others adapted quite fluently to changing price ratios, examples being John Arkwright grassing down one of the Hampton Court farms during the early nineteenth-century depression and Thomas Crewdson bringing in more beef and dairy cattle to Syde, Gloucestershire, in the later depression.

Richard Arkwright bought about 6000 acres at Hampton Court, Leominster, in 1809. In this case we do know something of the seller. He was the Fifth Earl of Essex, who had not even visited the property for a couple of years and had acquired it merely as part of an inheritance from his maternal grandmother, a Coningsby. The Earl was grateful enough to adopt her surname but not grateful enough to hold on to her property. He sold off small lots in the 1790s and others close to Hampton Court in 1807, when Thomas Berington from the neighbouring estate bought some of them. The Earl was more interested in his home at Little Cassiobury, Hertfordshire, where he was having a new mansion built by the fashionable architect, James Wyatt, and the grounds landscaped by the even more fashionable gardener, Humphrey Repton. This all cost money and the Earl therefore found his sales in Herefordshire highly convenient.

Later, Richard Arkwright's grandson encouraged a friend from Wigan to buy an estate in Herefordshire too. He was Elias Chadwick, younger son of Elias Chadwick, cotton manufacturer, thread maker and dealer and coal owner, of Swinton Hall, Lancashire. The younger Chadwick was educated at Worcester College, Oxford, and became a JP and DL for Herefordshire, besides being a magistrate in Lancashire. He built a new house—highly castellated and possibly reflecting the architecture of Hampton Court—at Pudleston in 1846. Pudleston had been sold to Elias Chadwick when the last of the old Herefordshire Duppa family died; who were the executors and beneficiaries of that family does not appear. Pudleston later went out of the Chadwick family in turn and a descendant became an organic gardener in California.

Sir Thomas Bazley was an exceptionally interesting individual. He was the son of a cotton manufacturer but founded his own business and made it the world's largest manufacturer of fine cotton and lace thread. He established estates in Gloucestershire, Hertfordshire (sic) and Oxfordshire, and after living near Moreton-in-Marsh bought a total of 5000 acres in the Fairford district of Gloucestershire in 1867. His son was educated at Cambridge and installed at Hatherop Castle. Soon after arriving in the district and during the 1870s, Bazley caused better cottages and solid, expensive-looking farmhouses in Cotswold stone to appear on his estate, where they may still be seen. This was very business-like, although it happened to be just in time for the Great Depression, when so much of the area 'tumbled down' to grass and farms were given up. Nevertheless the Bazleys survived the downturn and were able to retain the Hatherop estate for 130 years.

In many ways Sir Thomas was an outstanding liberal reformer who had established, with his business partner, a model nonsectarian industrial community at Barrow Bridge near Bolton in the 1830s and later became a Liberal MP, as well as DL of Lancashire. He was active in the Anti-Corn Law League, as befitted an industrialist who may have noticed (as others certainly did) that the high price of a pre-Repeal loaf raised his wage bill.

Despite his background, Bazley was exceptionally attracted to rural life, a love apparently so out of character that it 'bemused' radical Lancastrian visitors to his estates. Paradoxically, given his attraction to the countryside, his death in 1885 was at his summer residence at Lytham St Anne's. His descendants followed the typical course of successful moneyed families, being educated at public schools and making socially elevated marriages, although they sold the Hatherop estate in 2002.

It is difficult to isolate the elements in landowner behaviour because economic conditions, non-agricultural capital, family structures and individual attitudes were simultaneous influences. Richard Arkwright's son, John, was at first rather bored by farming but in the early 1840s took to it with a will. The prospects for agriculture were better than they had been in the 1820s and 1830s and after his father's death in 1843 John had much more capital to play with. He used it to undertake improvements on the estate. Incomers from industry typically had the advantage of wealth. A stress on the shortage of capital among Herefordshire farmers is palpable in the documents and was forthrightly asserted by J. B. Turner in a letter to the *Hereford Journal*. Turner thought landowners would have to make up for the lack by funding improvements, although not all were willing to do so. Much of their investment went into unproductive show, such as park walls and other embellishments, quite apart from expenditure on mansions. As to prospective tenant farmers, owners and their agents tended to assess them according to the capital they were thought to have, which in Herefordshire was likely to be judged by the number of cattle in their pastures; farmers' husbandry prowess seems to have been taken for granted, although agents were likely to have gleaned something about their ability.

With money from the cotton trade, John Arkwright was able to become a prominent agriculturist in the county, as was Thomas Andrew Knight, the pomologist, in his case using money made by an iron-mining ancestor. The Knight family from Worcestershire and the other great West Midland ironmaster family, the Foleys from Shropshire, had not been drawn to Herefordshire in the first instance by its agricultural prospects. The Knights had a forge on their Downton Castle estate and the Foleys bought land around Stoke Edith as early as 1670 because it was extensively timbered and might serve to supply the charcoal iron industry. Therefore, not quite all industrial money entering the region had done so exclusively for the standard reasons of status, amenity and investment inherent in owning farmland. These reasons had however always attracted London money and it was when they were making great fortunes in the nineteenth century that Lancastrian and other northern industrialists responded to similar social incentives.

Nor was it the case that all incomers lacked previous local connections. The Arkwrights had no prior involvement with Herefordshire, nor had Bazley with Gloucestershire, but the history on the surface is not always what it seems. We saw that J. B. Turner of Brockmanton proved to have a family connection with Manchester cotton. Similarly, William Higginson, whose fortune came from coal mining and who bought the sizeable Saltmarshe estate, Bromyard, from the Earl of Essex as early as 1799, was related to the old local gentry family of Barneby. He eventually left the estate to his nephew, Edmund Barneby, on condition that Edmund change his surname to Higginson.

Either way, the influx of industrial money eventually inspired a reaction. In 1904, Christopher Hatton Turnor (1873–1940), owner of stupendously vast estates in Lincolnshire, joined with the large Gloucestershire landowner, Charles Bathurst, MP (later Lord Bledisloe) to found the Central Landowners' Association. Their goal was to counteract what they saw as a threat to the traditional role of the aristocracy from the plutocracy of financiers and industrialists. This indicates that assimilation was not always as smooth as it seems on the surface. Turnor in particular was an agricultural reformer who thought that landowners should not subsidise their tenants by remitting rents in bad years but offer constructive economic and scientific advice instead. His ideas were a curate's egg—on the one hand defending large landowners and fixed class positions but on the other recommending smaller Danish-style farms backed by agrarian cooperatives and rural education. His schemes did not catch on either with other landowners or the voting public.

The plutocracy that offended established owners such as Turnor and Bathurst had never presented a fixed target. It was tempting for established owners to rail against successive parvenu cohorts but they could not halt the business of acquiring estates or creating new ones by buying farms and amalgamating them. As we have seen, the entrants assumed the guise, manners and attitudes of existing proprietors and from our distance in time became rather quickly, in the unavoidable phrase, as to the manor born. Entrants commonly 'married in' and if some chose 'unsuitable' women, their spouses had every incentive to learn. Richard Arkwright's son, Robert, married an actress—a niece of Sarah Siddons, no less, which itself implied a species of aristocracy in the world of theatre—and was for a time out of favour with his family. But his wife was good at playing a role and so charmed aristocratic guests and her in-laws that Robert received as his inheritance Sutton Scarsdale, Derbyshire: 5500 acres adorned by a house described as on the scale and of the quality of Chatsworth. Friction in the assimilation process gave rise to many a comedy of manners but for any given family of entrants it seldom lasted long and overall did not stem the recurrent infusions of new blood and new money.

Admittedly unearned wealth encouraged occasional descendants to become wastrels (Peel's grandson gambled away the Drayton estate, Frerichs's grandson was the decadent poet, Eric Stenbock), but most became barely distinguishable from their predecessors on the land. After all, many of the old landowning families had once been newcomers themselves and had acquired their money outside agriculture. What made the people with huge industrial fortunes conspicuous was that there were so many of them entering the land in a fairly short period at the end of the nineteenth century. Turnor and Bathurst would have been more conscious of new entrants drawn in by cheap land than of the sporadic arrivals of previous times. Social ambition attracted new men into the countryside but it was their financial resources that were significant for an agricultural sector which even in good times may have been short of capital and definitely required cash injections for updating farmsteads to meet successive waves of new organisation and technology. Not all newcomers survived the vicissitudes that agriculture subsequently faced and some of the great houses built by the Lancastrian cotton masters joined the many country houses that were later demolished. Yet the 'invasion' may be seen as adding a sizeable nineteenth-century stratum to the old palimpsest of landed investment.

Sources and Further Reading

Green, J. (2008). *Changing scenes: Celebrating 150 years of the Tenbury Agricultural Society 1858–2008.* Tenbury Wells: Tenbury Agricultural Society.

Howe, A. C. (1984). *The cotton masters.* Oxford: Clarendon Press.

Johnson, B. (2014). *The Churchill factor.* London: Hodder & Stoughton.

Jones, E. L. (1967). Industrial capital and landed investment: The Arkwrights in Herefordshire, 1809–43. In E. L. Jones & G. E. Mingay (Eds.), *Land, labour and population in the industrial revolution* (pp. 48–71). London: Edward Arnold.

Jones, E. L. (2010). *Locating the industrial revolution: Inducement and response.* Singapore: World Scientific.

Keltner, D. (2016). *The power paradox: How we gain and lose influence.* London: Allen Lane.

Mackenzie, M. H. (1959). Bakewell mill and the Arkwrights. *Journal of the Derbyshire Archaeological and Natural History Society, LXXIX,* 62–64.

Marshall, J. D. (1987). *Lancashire.* Newton Abbot: David & Charles.

Moir, E. (1957). The gentlemen clothiers: A study of the organisation of the Gloucestershire cloth trade, 1750–1835. In H. P. R. Finberg (Ed.), *Gloucestershire studies.* Leicester: Leicester University Press.

Paintin, B. R. K. (1946). *'The temple of his grace': A survey of Wesleyan Methodism in Wherwell.* Privately Printed.

Procter, T. (2004). Two men of industry, many businesses. The Soho Firm of Matthew Boulton and James Watt as revealed by the archives of Soho. *Business Archives, 88,* 13–24.

Turnor, C. (1921). *The land and its problems.* London: Methuen.

Verey, D. (Ed.). (1983). *The diary of a Victorian Squire: Extracts from the diaries and letters of Dearman and Emily Birchall.* Gloucester: Alan Sutton.

Walton, J. K. (1987). *Lancashire: A social history 1558–1939.* Manchester: Manchester University Press.

CHAPTER 3

The Lower Orders

Abstract Rural workers were treated harshly and with disdain, indoors and out. Social apartheid was reinforced by segregating dwellings and reorganising household layouts. Female domestic service expanded. Considerable evidence exists of poor treatment of employees, including sexual harassment; informal contact with servants was otherwise often avoided. The movement of labour towards industries, cities and the colonies was not sufficient to offset these effects or do much to raise wages.

Keywords Labour migration • Rural workforce • Sexual harassment • Social apartheid

The rural society ratified by the Restoration settlement was hierarchical to excess. Alongside it developed a market town economy whose inhabitants remained significantly dependent on the patronage and purchasing by local landowners. This patronage did not fade until the late eighteenth century, when the genteel began to buy their provisions from London and spend more time and money in the capital or fashionable spa towns. The market towns suffered from this diversion of cash, although some of their inhabitants, often nonconformists and Quakers, managed to preserve a dignified independence within their own circles. As for the landed estates surrounding the towns, Roman Catholic authors, hostile to the rise of Protestant landowners grown fat on monastic property after the Dissolution, criticised the new geography beginning to emerge as early as the sixteenth century. They depicted quitting the old manor houses next to the churches in favour of mansions isolated in parkland as a withdrawal from community. There was indeed such a movement. The aim was to secure privacy for the landowners, a vogue that really seized them from the eighteenth century onwards. Within doors, seclusion from the servants and retreat from a stream of guests was prized by landowning families. The leading country house architect of the mid-nineteenth century, William Burn, was noted for the way his designs achieved this interior isolation.

A movement to shift their houses away from the villages likewise occurred among farmers, whose numbers in lowland England shrank towards a coterie of rich tenants. They or their landlords built the Georgian farms of brick and tile that stand alone in what were then newly enclosed fields. There was some sense to this from the farming point of view but it was also social separatism. Farming created its own self-referring community and a degree of comfortable living that persists today. The old timber-and-thatch farmhouses on the village street were split into cottages for farm workers, though today some of them have been amalgamated again as residences for retirees and weekenders.

Estate landscapes expanded and parks became more numerous. Villagers who were not to the taste of the lord of the manor, or more likely his agent, could be excluded. 'Closed' villages appeared, where no one from elsewhere could gain a settlement entitling them to poor relief. They were the reverse of 'open' villages—'all liberty and swearing', as Richard Jefferies sardonically observed—that could not police themselves in the same way and where cheap housing was crammed in, often gable-end on to the road, to rent out to labourers. As a result farm hands, little children among them, were often obliged to walk miles from these dormitories to work on the farms of distant estates.

The processes whereby landowner families dissociated themselves from village society, other than to recruit servants, exacted a price from society. One aspect of this arose from the growing seclusion of their parks, policies, streams and woodlands. These they came to defend sternly and often viciously against trespass, fishing and poaching, the gathering of fuel and wild products and simple access. As far back as 1655 the Penruddock conspirators against Cromwell had deluded themselves that more people agreed with them and were willing to take up arms than proved to be so. Landowners regarded the last labourers' revolt in 1830 with comparable dismay. They had presided over patriarchal societies and mistaken deference for approval; they were especially furious that tradesmen and artisans, who had some small property and hence a little stake in society, tended to be ringleaders in the revolt. Villagers in turn, spotting that the Anglican incumbents sided with the landowners, left the church in disgust. Thereafter, where labourers and small tradesmen were able to acquire scraps of land, they built the chapels of the nonconformist sects that proliferated in Victorian England. These acts of defiance, under the noses of the established church, imposed their own costs: men who worked on the estate could lose their jobs and some were obliged or decided it was politic to emigrate. Most such cases have gone unrecorded but there were examples at Wherwell, Hampshire, and Idbury, Oxfordshire.

After the 1830s villagers began more actively to move away from the countryside to London and the industrial towns, or the colonies, in search of work and independence. This was a species of revenge in itself and in 1840 Wiltshire became the first county to record an absolute fall of population. By mid-century farmers began to fear the draught of labour shortages. They exaggerated the shortfall but its reality did oblige them to pay a little higher wages. The men who quit were understandably the more independent-minded, as well no doubt as the more disgruntled. Both the independent and the resentful were likely to have been among the most capable workers.

The slight outmigration in the middle of the nineteenth century and the consequent minor decline in the supply of workers were however soon offset by the slumping demand for labour during the arable depression of the final decades. An unsolved puzzle is why labour did not move out and emigrate more boldly: arable areas were depressed, fields abandoned and cottages decayed, and still the fundamental equilibrium was not overthrown. The young and energetic moved away. They left behind them (once the franchise had been extended) villages full of 'deference voters' who proved willing to vote for their employers against their own interests. This servile habit became a trademark of the nineteenth and early twentieth centuries, distinguishing southern English people from those in the large cities. If deference voting had a rationale it was the feeble one that the employing classes could understand public affairs whereas ordinary people could not, something that would not have been surprising given the limited education provided for most people.

The unpleasant treatment of indoor staff was particularly hard for employees to escape. This was so even leaving out of account well-documented, though surely exceptional, cases where servants in the largest houses were expected to flatten themselves against the walls, creep into corners and generally make themselves invisible when the master passed by. The digging of tunnels where servants could go about their tasks unseen was not unknown. Staff could always be summoned by one of the bells hanging in a row downstairs. One extreme case of this aloofness was the Duke of Portland, politely described as reclusive, who built tunnels under Welbeck Abbey, Nottinghamshire, in order that his staff might avoid him. Another case was that of the domineering woman who owned Shibden Hall, Yorkshire, and built a tunnel to keep her servants out of sight. The long stone passage to the servants' quarters in the basement of a house at Lyndhurst, Hampshire, supposedly gave Lewis Carroll the idea of the white rabbit scuttling into a hole in the ground. The flats at Faringdon House, Oxfordshire, were reached by a long corridor through a 'downstairs' painted in institutional colours, not the cream tone of 'upstairs', and with concrete floors instead of parquet. None of the tenants were permitted to walk in front of the house or intrude on the notice of its occupants. That was in 1987.

Humiliation was most complete for the black slave children kept as toys by eighteenth-century aristocrats but was by no means reserved for them. Other servants might find themselves kept at arms' length. In the seventeenth century employers were already being recommended to keep their own offspring away from all but an approved cadre of servants whose accents would not be too catching and who could be relied on not to fill their heads with the superstitious pronouncements that passed for knowledge in the cottages. Although the opportunity to discriminate among types of servant depended on having a large enough establishment, other means of introducing social distance between employers' children and menials were not hard to find. The Victorian insistence on uniforms for servants reduced their individuality. It was not necessarily resented. People who grew up 'in service' and whose whole life it was could be more than accepting of social hierarchy, happy to defend it and to identify with their employing family's interests.

Social apartheid persists in modern England, however smoothed over by gentlemanly manners and master-man closeness. Ample research, for instance by the Sutton Trust, demonstrates the inequality of access to the best-resourced education. At least inequality no longer extends to depersonalising domestic servants in order to save their employers the trouble of remembering their birth names. Formerly, household functionaries were known only by their first names and labelled in stereotyped ways. Footmen were John, Charles or James and a serving woman called

Mary might have to become something else if the lady of the house were herself a Mary. The proliferation of rather fancy Christian names among the late nineteenth-century working class was resisted, so that when a boy called Gerald was hired at Blenheim he reports he was renamed Johnny. Only the heads of each branch of household staff, the butler and the housekeeper, were accorded their own names and the courtesy of a title. Even in Kelmscott Manor—not that it really was a manor—belonging to the champagne socialist, William Morris, one female servant plucked out of a pub was always demeaned as 'Red Lion Mary'. The practice of renaming indoor servants later spread from the great houses to the farms.

During the nineteenth century, population growth and grossly overcrowded cottages pushed working-class girls into service in ever larger proportions, until a staggering total of almost 40 per cent of the occupied female workforce was employed in personal service by 1911. That census year saw the number of gamekeepers at its peak and represented the high tide of estate employment. The misallocation of resources away from productive labour will be plain. Domestic service had spread to lower and lower classes of employer—all seeking status—and to ever smaller houses. Small households made close contact with the servants hard to avoid and from them, as well as from country houses, is recorded the whole gamut of human behaviour and interpersonal relations ranging from kindly to atrocious. The often disdainful treatment of staff and the control to which they were subjected are described in the reminiscences of former servants that began to appear during the second half of the twentieth century, though a few earlier ones do exist. The shocking exploitation of domestic staff has now been graphically demonstrated by Dr. Pamela Cox in a BBC2 television series called *Servants: The True Story of Life Below Stairs*. She illustrates the apartheid between employer and employee in the nineteenth century, intensified by the increased hiring of servants in small town houses where the mistress was keen to insist on a social distance between the classes even though this was harder to maintain than in stand-alone country houses.

The sexual attentions foisted on female servants cannot be accurately measured, being covert, but enough glimpses survive to reveal it was not rare. Flagrant examples are recorded at all periods. In the 1640s Henry Marten's orgies notoriously made the Vale of White Horse ring. David Hackett Fischer's study of seventeenth-century Virginia shows the prevalence of illicit sex between unequals there, in translocated southern English society. John Aubrey's *Brief Lives* drops more than hints. The diaries of

Samuel Pepys and Robert Hooke both show what a determined lecher might achieve. In her biography of Pepys Claire Tomalin comments that servant girls must have been used to being manhandled and often 'simply accepted that this was part of the scheme of things'. And Roger Longrigg describes a late eighteenth-century landowner in Shropshire who installed in little cottages dotted about his estate country girls by whom he had a large number of children. He was hardly the only man to take advantage of his position.

The eighteenth century produced the licentiousness of the Hellfire Club, Lord Cobham's Temple of Venus at Stowe with its couches and murals of sexy scenes from *The Faerie Queene,* the Rococco gardens at Painswick and (in Scotland) the Benison Club. Recent books on garden history delight in tales about the debauchery. Then, in nineteenth-century England, came the deadening influence of the Evangelicals, who just before Victoria's reign were already starting to change more than surface expressions of morality. Darwin's eldest daughter, of all people, made a pastime of hunting for stinkhorns, *Phallus impudicus,* which according to her niece, Gwen Raverat, were burned 'in the deepest secrecy on the drawing room fire with the door locked—because of the morals of the maids'. The aim of employers was to police personal behaviour and relations among their staff, which not only chimed with contemporary moral thinking but was in their own interest because it helped retain people they had trained. Charles a Court, writing from Heytesbury in 1825, declared that with the wrong arrangement of entrances to servants' bedrooms, 'depend upon it every housemaid will be with child within the twelvemonth. I have some experience this way, having been obliged to dismiss two excellent servants, owing to their being in contact with the men servants'.

As public opinion became ever more censorious with respect to casual relationships in their own class, the sons, nephews and male friends of employing families increasingly directed their attempts at liaison towards the servants. Despite the repressive times, deflowering the maids continued to be a sport in some households. The danger to employers was that a son of the household might contract to marry a maid servant, as did happen, although very rarely. Maybe attitudes began to alter a little at the end of the nineteenth century, when sophisticated people started to feel that mid-Victorian sensibilities were faintly ridiculous and, as Mark Girouard writes in *Life in the English Country House,* the fact of a little discreet upper-class adultery along bedroom corridors became an open secret. Constraints on landowner behaviour were merely conventions and when they were relaxed the result could be a barnyard, like the promiscuity of rich emigres in the 'Happy Valley' of Kenya during the 1920s and 1930s.

The moral panic of today assumes that each and every relationship between individuals of unequal power and prestige is one of men imposing themselves on unwilling females, regardless of the facts that women and girls can flirt too and their ranks always contained a number of tuft hunters. What kept fornication in check was the ironclad rule that the women took the blame. This made many reluctant to play ball, whatever their urges. Nevertheless mothers were disposed to sack the prettier maids when their sons reached an impressionable age. Builders were employed to put what was called a 'trick step' on the wooden treads of servants' staircases—four steps from the bottom was a step two inches higher than the others. It was something like the Nightingale floor in a Tokugawa Japanese house, a warning signal, although the threat was different.

The broadcaster, Monty Don, found among the tiny, plain rooms for servants at the top of a house one room that was big enough only for a bed, with its walls and ceilings decorated by elaborate mouldings. It was in order that the owner could claim *droit de seigneur* over the maid of his choice. That was in modern France. It differed from arrangements in English country houses only in its explicitness, although even there cases can be found of private staircases leading to the servants' sleeping quarters. They were bridgeheads across a divide otherwise scarcely to be passed. 'It can still be a disconcerting experience', says Girouard, 'to push through the baize doors, studded with brass nails, that divided the servants from the family, and pass from carpets, big rooms, light, comfort and air to dark corridors, linoleum, poky rooms, and the ghostly smell of stale cabbage'. This was what M. R. D. Foot found at Chatsworth in 1948, where the servants' floor was utterly Spartan and illuminated only by skylights—no windows, because it was deemed unsuitable for servants to look down on their betters.

The estate system was cold and cruel, however warmed by discretionary acts of charity and bowls of soup carried to sick villagers by landowners' wives or daughters. Mary Sturge Gretton, writing about Barrington on the Cotswolds, observes that the birthdays of the sisters who presided over 'their' village remained red-letter days in the local children's calendar because on summer anniversaries the village children were taken to walk about the park. 'There is something about this reminiscence', says Mrs. Gretton, '—its fragility, so meagre a treat producing so full-bodied an ecstasy—that preserves a real aroma from a world that is gone'. She was writing in 1914, when that austere world was barely on the brink of passing away.

Property, not people, was the watchword. Parks were surrounded by brick or stone walls that cost fortunes to build and where the gate pillars alone might cost more than the house of an employee. Cottages were dwarfed not merely by the local mansion but by vast kennels and stables that indicated the landowner's priorities. The discrepancy extended to relative details, such as the provision of felt under the roofs of animal housing on tenanted farms whereas the roofs of labourers' cottages might be left unprotected. It was indicative of landowners' priorities that the Earl of Craven had built Ashdown House (then Berkshire, now Oxfordshire), as a hunting lodge for his presumed mistress, Elizabeth the Winter Queen, but a later seventeenth-century Earl provided only the minute cottages for workers that may still be seen in the Craven village of Uffington. Overcrowding in small cottage properties could become intense and especially so given the large families of Victorian times. This made it understandable why village wives competed to find places as domestic servants for their daughters of twelve or thirteen, where they might be fed and kept apart from the premature solicitations of the local hobbledy-hoys. The mothers of the little girls presumably discounted any danger from employers or their sons.

It was a dog-eat-dog society. One outside observer, Prince Hermann von Puckler-Muskau, who visited a very large number of parks and gardens in the 1820s, found the English upper class to be 'hard, exclusive and often philistine'. Commercial risk was passed down from landowners to tenant farmers. The farmers passed on what costs they could to the ratepayers or the farm labourers, who might be stood off at will and left without work in the coldest seasons. In some areas the task of supplying labour was outsourced to gangmasters. Hours of work were immensely long, as were many journeys to work; turning up for work was mandatory. As a Duke of Marlborough said, 'the lower orders are never ill'.

Before poor law 'reform' in 1836 parishes had supplied houses for their paupers; William Cobbett named the individual people living in those at Hurstbourne Tarrant, Hampshire, which were the worst he had ever seen. When village poor houses were replaced by centralised union workhouses, those unfortunates who just managed to keep out of the 'grubbers' (as the workhouses were known) found themselves obliged to seek accommodation in the 'mud towns' of some nearby market town. The cottages of employees who remained in the villages were also of unreliable quality and perhaps badly maintained: about 1900 a shepherd was born at Daglingworth, Gloucestershire, in a house with so leaky a roof that an umbrella was held over his mother while she gave birth. Children thought themselves lucky to get employment in stone picking. Anyone who reads widely in parish histories or talks to old country dwellers will learn of instances like these. There are so many that it is needless to document them.

Examples of actual cruelty are legion, although books of local or social history continue to make the reality seem more remote or more benign than it was. The history of rural England is commonly written in nostalgic vein, as if man's inhumanity to man has ended and need be deplored only from a position of Olympian detachment. The social historians of R. H. Tawney's day have been replaced by economic historians who compress history into abstractions and might be accused of viewing the past through the wrong end of the telescope. No moral stance is taken where one is needed. The horrors of past poverty are remote from their experience; they scarcely notice the submerged poverty in today's countryside. The prosperity is so much more visible. Modern academics have suburban upbringings and can look on rustic indignities like anthropologists viewing foreign tribes, which might be more acceptable if injustice did not linger at home. Dispassionate analysis is a proper professional goal but assumptions need to be relaxed and abstractions given faces to allow the individuals of the past to re-emerge. That should not be impossible. Cruelty affected the forebears of the very people who now search out their family histories in the record offices or return from former colonies to trace their genealogy.

Into the twentieth century, landowners continued to sit on the magistrate's bench and sentence their hungry neighbours to hard labour or the treadmill for inconceivably trivial offences against property. Half-a-century earlier they transported them to Botany Bay for even less; the man traps in museums are signs of how harshly they prosecuted the war against poachers. Suppressing the pleasures of the poor was commonplace and it is clear that popular activities involving the abuse of animals, such as bull-baiting or cockfighting, were forbidden by law without similar sanctions being applied to the otter hunts or *battue* shoots of the rich. Village alehouses could be shut down with no repercussions on the conviviality of the wine-drinkers up at the hall. John Keble, author of the leading Victorian best-seller, *The Christian Year*, was associated with a local Gloucestershire landowner in a proposal to do away with the alehouses. In Hampshire, where this campaign was particularly strong, the poor sometimes outfoxed their superiors by organising 'help ales', where a group of friends combined to buy a barrel of beer and drink it on a Saturday evening in one of their own houses.

As Keble's example begins to indicate, the clergy were deeply implicated in the harshness of the past. Their role was to acclimatise people to the system, not to challenge it, nor to smooth over its asperities in any profound fashion. Some of them were the younger sons of landowners and mingled socially with the class into which they had been born. Some were 'squarsons', keener on organised hunts than organised charity. Some were slave owners, as can be seen in the lists published by University College, London, of people lavishly compensated for their losses from the repeal of the slave trade. One dispute about the condition of agricultural labour involved the charge by William Cobbett that prominent opponents of slavery, like William Wilberforce, paid attention to that grotesque injustice but not to the plight of the workers on English estates, who may have had freedom but not much more than freedom to starve. Two wrongs do not make a right but Cobbett had a point. Relieving the poverty of the English poor systematically rather than ad hoc was a neglected duty.

Accordingly, what one sees is a rural society endlessly reproducing its divisions and oppressions, and not exporting enough of its labour force to raise the standard of living more than a fraction. Improvements in well-being did occur in the third quarter of the nineteenth century but they were slight and never dramatic. For centuries, rural England housed a population that experienced—was buffeted, if you will—by the shocks and shifts in the larger society. From time to time, depressions in agriculture might push down the returns to owning land, but the estate system endured and was repeatedly added to by capital from London, Lancashire or the colonies. This continual, if not exactly continuous, inflow of funds was what ensured the system's long life and produced path-dependency. After 1660 the rulers of rural society were never again challenged and never again confronted themselves, there was no meaningful social or political competition, and landlords and squires continued to be cocks o' the walk. Stripped of particular events, rationalisations, defences and detail, the history of landed society was of an abidingly unequal system modified by little more than the rise and fall of individual families.

SOURCES AND FURTHER READING

Bourne, G. (1912). *Change in the village*. London: Duckworth.

Bourne, G. (1983). *Memoirs of a Surrey labourer*. London: Breslich and Foss.

Buckmaster, J. (1982). *A village politician*. Horsham: Calban Books.

Burnett, J. (Ed.). (1974). *Useful Toil: Autobiographies of working people from the 1870s to the 1920s*. London: Allen Lane.

Cobbett, W. (1912). *Rural rides*. London: J. M. Dent & Sons.

Don, M. (2014). *A French garden journey*. London: Simon & Schuster.

Fischer, D. H. (1969). *Albion's seed*. Oxford: Oxford University Press.

Geddes, A. (n.d.). *Samuel Best and the Hampshire labourer*. Andover: Local History Society.

Girouard, M. (1980). *Life in the English country house*. Harmondsworth: Penguin.

Gretton, M. S. (1914). *A corner of the Cotswolds through the nineteenth century*. London: Methuen.

Hammond, J. L., & Hammond, B. B. (1948). *The village labourer*. London: Guild Books.

Holmes a Court, Charles, Heytesbury letters. 2/12/1825. www.holmesacourt. org/hac/Heytesburyletters/letterindex.htm

Jackman, N., & Quinn, T. (2012). *The Cook's tale: Life below stairs as it really was*. London: Coronet.

Jaeger, M. (1967). *Before Victoria*. Harmondsworth: Penguin.

Jones, E. L. (1964). The agricultural labour market in England, 1793–1872. *Economic History Review, XVII*(2), 322–338.

Jones, E. (2014). Sources of protein for rural people in Richard Jefferies' Day. *The Richard Jefferies Society Journal, 26*, 35–53.

Longrigg, R. (1977). *The English squire and his sport*. London: Michael Joseph.

Malcolmson, R. W. (1979). *Popular recreations in English society 1700–1850*. Cambridge: Cambridge University Press.

Markham, S. (1990). *A testimony of her times: Based on Penelope Hind's diaries and correspondence 1787–1838*. Salisbury: Michael Russell.

Neeson, J. M. (1996). *Commoners: Common right, enclosure and social change in England, 1700–1820*. Cambridge: Cambridge University Press.

Parshall, L. B. (Ed.). (2016). *Letters of a dead man*. Cambridge, MA: Harvard University Press.

Pevsner, N. (1953). *Nottinghamshire*. Harmondsworth: Penguin.

Raverat, G. (1960). *Period piece: A Cambridge childhood*. London: Faber and Faber.

Stead, D. R. (2006). Delegated risk in English agriculture 1750–1850, the labour market. *Labour History Review, 71*(2), 128–144.

Swinford, G. (1987). *The jubilee boy*. Filkins: The Filkins Press.

Tempero, D. J. (n.d.). *They simply stole to live… cases before the Andover courts 1829–1851*. Andover: Andover Advertiser.

Tomalin, C. (2002). *Samuel Pepys: The unequalled self*. Leicester: W. F. Howes.

Trigg, D. A. (1998). *Salt of the earth: The life and work of bygone farm labourers*. London: Minerva Press.

Williamson, J. G. (1987). Did English factor markets fail during the industrial revolution. *Oxford Economic Papers, 39*, 641–678.

Williamson, J. G. (1994). Leaving the farm to go to the city: Did they leave quickly enough? In J. A. James & M. Thomas (Eds.), *Capitalism in context* (159–182). Chicago: University of Chicago Press.

CHAPTER 4

Expelling the People

Abstract Extensive land remodelling took place, especially in the eighteenth and nineteenth centuries. Prominent aims were to secure privacy for landowners and improve the view from their houses. The process sometimes involved the actual demolition of entire villages and occasionally their rebuilding on new sites. An associated development was the erection of long, high walls around parkland. Many landowners did lose out during the arable depression of the late nineteenth century and the two world wars of the twentieth century but were replaced by the newly moneyed. In any case country house building has since revived.

Keywords Amenity motive • Country House building • Landscape remodelling • Park walls • Privacy motive • Village demolition

While he was still a boy, Frederick I of Prussia was given a regiment of soldiers—some say children, others say dwarves—which he drilled up and down like the Grand Old Duke of York. Prince William, son of Queen Anne, had his own regiment of ninety boys before he died at the age of eleven. Dominance and control over the lives of others seem extraordinarily appealing to a majority of those with power, and none more so than the English landed classes. Here are three examples: first, William

Amcotts-Ingilby demolished the village of Ripley, near Harrogate, in the 1850s and rebuilt it on the lines of somewhere he had seen in Alsace. When a child ran out and caused his horse to throw him, he forbade the villagers to use their front doors; secondly, between 1885 and 1900 the Rothschilds superimposed a model village of tied cottages for estate workers on the old village of Ashton, East Northamptonshire; thirdly, James Ismay, lord of the manor of Iwerne Minster, Dorset, in the 1920s, wanted to develop a model village. His ambition extended to a uniform for the children of the inhabitants: authoritarians are attracted to uniformity and do not like other people to have choices. Ismay obliged the boys to wear red jumpers with a blue band and the girls to wear Little Red Riding Hood cloaks, as if they were his own army of little soldiers. His paternalism may have been extreme, but intervention in the lives of those they considered their social inferiors was endemic in the countryside for centuries.

One form that paternalism commonly took was dictating where people might live, a practice that surprisingly often included moving the sites of villages holus-bolus. It was part of the ruthless alterations of countryside and property that continued under the hands of landowners at successive periods. The changes have often been studied but usually with respect to single episodes like the enclosures for sheep in the late Middle Ages or of the common fields in the eighteenth century. The phases are seldom treated as inherent in the system, in the landlord class's increasing monopolisation of the countryside, which is to say as expressions of a perennial urge to reshape the land according to ever-evolving prospects and fashions.

The argument might be that because the villages belonged to the proprietors they had a right to do with them what they wished. Few were likely to dissent from this in the eighteenth century, when the saying was that 'Property had been erected as King', but the process still interfered with people's lives. Admittedly, once feudalism had died, villagers could move away, as increasing numbers did, but for most people there was no prudent alternative to accepting their lot. Church teaching reinforced the obedience inculcated by village society. In *All Things Bright and Beautiful* from Mrs. Alexander's *Hymns for Little Children* of 1848, the verse which proclaims 'The rich man in his castle, The poor man at his gate, God made them high and lowly, And ordered their estate', was still sung in primary schools a century later. In this atmosphere, arbitrarily moving houses and their occupants about like pieces in a board game was nothing exceptional.

Expanding the estate system by various means continued over the centuries, ensuring that ownership came into fewer and fewer hands. In the Middle Ages the assertion of possession could be violent and the threat of violence persisted in later times when resistance was in practice reduced to grousing. Medieval property was by no means as secure as it was to become—property was, so to speak, not yet 'erected as King'—and was vulnerable to actual fighting among members of the elite. During the 1540s and early 1550s a few bishops wished to repeal the land transactions that had followed the Dissolution, and the resultant rumblings and incidents were enough to alarm lay owners about the security of their ownership. Jennifer Loach's study of the reign of Mary Tudor claims that 'so embedded did this anxiety become amongst the English landed classes that it could still be played upon by the Whig pamphleteers of the 1670s and 1680s'. Men who bought land could seldom be sure that the vendor would not reappear to challenge their ownership. The fear of long trailing claims meant the lineage of ancient ownership was likely to be recited far into the future, as when the early seventeenth-century names 'Stratton Jones' or 'Stratton late Jones' were rehearsed in legal documents relating to Stratton St Margaret, Wiltshire, more than a century after the Jones family had sold out.

Back in the 1440s, the Pastons, whose letters have survived, did not have a secure hold on their manor of Gresham, Norfolk. Lord Moleyns, who was Robert Hungerford from the influential Wiltshire family of sheep-masters, put in a claim for it. The Pastons' house was seized by servants he sent for the purpose; they cut loopholes through which to fire handguns, for the fifteenth century was not only on the cusp of law and order but also on the cusp of the new technology of gunpowder. The history of this family also shows that, whereas private property might be physically contested, public property was more easily usurped: when they wanted a road moved for their personal convenience in 1444, all that was needed was the consent of an important local figure, in this case the priest.

The ruthlessness underpinning the Arcadian beauty of estate landscapes was made plain in the next century by the behaviour of William Herbert, first Earl of Pembroke. He was one of the thrusting Welshmen who had followed the Tudor, Henry VII, and were called the 'Taffia'. They came to seize any opportunities that England offered. On the Dissolution of the Monasteries, Herbert was granted the lands of the abbey of Wilton, near Salisbury. To enlarge his park he simply erased the village of Washern; he took over the common fields and even land held in severalty, that is to say, in the possession of individuals. Those who were ousted were compensated, but not generously enough to replace the income stream offered by farming one's own land. The times were ones of pressure on means of subsistence and the inhabitants of Washern were among the distressed folk who rose in revolt in 1549. While Herbert was away in Glamorgan, they set about re-erecting their demolished houses. We know this because John Paston (strangely enough) happened to report that Sir William Herbert's park had been 'plucked down' by the commoners. Then Herbert returned, bringing with him his Welsh tenants, and 'slew to death divers of the rebels'—hunting them down and murdering them on the sites of their own homes. The king himself recorded the fact, apparently without demur. Adam Nicolson tellingly comments that 'the essence of Arcadia is that it belongs to the winners... The underlying meaning of parkland is as a reward for victory'.

If we pass on to the seventeenth century, arbitrary demolitions did not cease, some still being undertaken medieval-fashion to ease the development of deer parks. Nor did families who became prominent Cromwellians fail to join in the activities. In the late 1620s or early 1630s, Henry Ludlow (a member of the regicide's Edmund Ludlow's family) pulled down the small village of Tadley, Hampshire, including the church house. In 1634 a group of the inhabitants of Tadley brought an action against him whereby 'articles of misdeameanours and oppression [were] complained of to the Council [of the Star Chamber] by Ralph Hillier and divers other poor people, inhabitants of Tadley'. The complaints, detailed in the Calendar of State Papers Domestic for 1634, included the withholding of wages, failing to attend the hearing of the Assizes about this, delaying the payment of parish rates, threatening the collectors, procuring witnesses to commit perjury against the poor people who complained about him and pulling down 'ten or twelve houses in Tadley and Pamber, one of them being the Church-house, the rent thereof went towards the repairing of the Parish Church'. Local resistance did no good; Tadley Place still stands, the church still stands, but the site of the village is vacant to this day.

The motive for this demolition was probably to acquire the sites and farm plots rather than through a desire for privacy, because (as the local historian, Alan Albery, suggested when he showed me the site) Ludlow had permitted the hamlet to stand for another thirty or forty years after erecting Tadley Place, his own new house nearby. By that time, however, the desire for the seclusion of their dwellings on the part of landowners was becoming more and more apparent. It may be that rich incomers could now afford to be concerned as much with amenities as with the productivity of their farms. The extension of parks can sometimes be detected in the ridge-and-furrow under the grassy stretches, and this had ordinarily imposed an agricultural cost. The rage for amenities meant that landowners were prepared to bear it.

Nationally, demolitions continued, although the opportunity for further destruction was reduced because the stock of villages was smaller than it had been. This was thanks to the extensive clearing of medieval villages brought to notice by that pioneer of landscape history, the late Maurice Beresford. A not uncommon feature of deserted villages, in Beresford's view, was a great house standing alone in its park, bearing the name of some former parish and accompanied within the park walls by a lonely parish church. But even Great Homer nods and in his research Beresford underplays the number of post-medieval losses, reaching this conclusion by two routes. First, he concentrates on the Midlands and North, which for him happened to be within easiest reach and where evictions in favour of sheep had been at their peak. This deflects his enquiry away from the later imparking by newly moneyed families around London, to which they wished to retain access. Beresford claims that only a small number of villages were erased, mainly in the eighteenth century, for reasons of 'beauty and utility'—utility for whom, it might be asked. Secondly, Beresford does not count a village as 'lost' where a replacement was built outside the park pale, a definition that minimises the sense of disruption and distracts attention from the game-of-monopoly aspect of landownership.

Undoubtedly some of the replacements were 'model villages', and the houses were likely to be of a higher standard than the antiquated dwellings they replaced. That the new cottages were superior to the old cannot however disguise the dictatorial fashion in which removals were carried out or hide the contrast between the cramped accommodation provided and the grand architecture of kennels and stables or the miles of estate walls. Some examples of enormous walls are Richmond Park, where Charles I's eight miles of high wall were long in contention; Fonthill, Wiltshire, where at the end of the eighteenth century William Beckford erected—depending on authority—a six-, seven- or eight-mile wall; Nuneham Courtenay, Oxfordshire, six-and-a-half miles of wall; and Charborough Park, Dorset, where in 1841–1842 the landowner had the new Wimborne-Dorchester turnpike moved further from his house and built a wall with over two million bricks. The only park wall that was not intrinsically hostile was the one, eight foot high and three miles long, with which Charles Waterton (1782–1865) surrounded his Yorkshire estate to create a nature reserve.

Not only were villages and roads shifted but churches might be also pulled down and replaced by new ones, or left stranded in the park. In the 1630s, while extending a deer park at Childersley, Cambridgeshire, not one but two churches were pulled down, to be replaced by a private chapel;

despite ecclesiastical protests the church income was 'diverted'. In 1636 two villages were demolished at Kirby Park, Leicestershire, to develop the mansion and park. The demolition of villages was on an expanded scale during the eighteenth and nineteenth centuries. The number of new parks in the Home Counties is understood to have virtually doubled between 1760 and 1820. Christopher Taylor says in *Village and Farmstead* that there were 'far more [clearances] than has been realized', with examples in every English county. In Northamptonshire, as an instance, eight villages were completely cleared between 1720 and 1850 and only one was replaced by a new settlement. A far greater number of villages (25) were altered in that county by imparking, which continued into the 1870s, and 'this partial destruction was probably much more widespread than we imagine'.

New 'extension' (of cultivation) farms are a familiar landscape feature, but they were typically situated on moors or downs, or were ring-fenced farms built out in the fields after Parliamentary enclosure. Unintentionally offsetting this new building, old-established farmsteads were sometimes expunged. Taylor cites a thirteenth-century farm in Northamptonshire that was pulled down by Sir Thomas Tresham in 1597 in favour of a garden for a new house. Taylor calls this an 'odd reason for a site being abandoned' whereas it seems nothing of the sort—the desire of the rich for ornamental grounds and vistas was a standard purpose of landscape engineering. Indeed, Taylor's several examples of village removals indicate that appearances were the customary motive. Some landowners could not leave well alone. In 1739 Thomas Anson shifted the village of Shugborough, Staffordshire, out of sight of his house, and early in the next century Thomas Lord Anson moved it again in order further to enlarge the park.

Taylor does wisely point out that demolitions can be mysterious, for the history of settlements is often obscure and some imparkings do seem to have followed a pre-existing shrinkage of villages (although the landowner may have previously bought up houses with their demolition in mind). Overall there was a sufficient array of village demolitions and a much larger one of partial clearances to show that numbers of landowners engaged in reshaping the environment to increase their personal pleasure, whatever inconvenience and upset it caused to others.

In the midst of these moves the inhabitants might be reassigned to a nearby settlement or even sent further away. They were put out of sight. At Stowe, Buckinghamshire, they were summarily distributed among the neighbouring villages, while at Trafalgar, Wiltshire, they were despatched across the river to settle in Charlton. Alan Albery has reprinted part of an unpublished account by the landowner, W. L. Wiggett Chute, of how he operated at Sherborne St. John, Hampshire: Chute wrote that in 1828, 'there was a nest of very bad old cottages at Pollard's End a long way from the church and school and a nuisance to everyone. These I was enabled to pull down having built many new cottages in different parts of [the] Parish. I was the more easily able to accomplish this by [the] sending out of two batches of Emigrants to Canada... Many of the worst and most idle characters in the parish then emigrated much to their own benefit and relief of the Parish'. Albery located the site of the vanished hamlet of Pollard's End and found it coincided with earthworks listed by Hampshire County Council as the site of medieval houses, although medieval rather misses the point.

Identifying and counting demolished villages or the imparking with which demolition was associated is both simple and difficult. Many examples can be discovered by working through the website of Parks & Gardens UK. Over thirty post-medieval cases readily appear in a total of fourteen counties lying in a great triangle between Dorset, Derbyshire and Cambridgeshire. There is no chance that this compilation is exhaustive because the removal of cottages in the course of imparking is not of foremost interest to parkland or garden enthusiasts. Nor was imparking necessarily completed all at once, for it was a slow job with pick and shovel. For example, although the itinerary of the self-styled 'place-maker', Capability Brown, as he travelled around a total of 200 estates is more or less known, the date of his descent on any given property may have meant only that he set the work in motion before moving on to begin another remodelling elsewhere. In his absence the actual landscaping may have continued for years. The inclusions of lost parks and gardens in the Parks and Gardens' list concentrate suspiciously on the Greater Manchester area, Shropshire and Worcestershire, as if the topic attracted the special attention of the compilers there without necessarily doing so elsewhere. In any case the relevant county is not always stated. When the pulling down of a village and perhaps its replacement outside the home park does receive a mention, details are often few, even when supplemented by a standard source like *British History Online* (itself inconsistent in what it covers) and by local histories. Nevertheless a sizeable role for demolition cannot be denied.

Motives for village demolition and removal shifted over time. Employees' cottages had typically been close to the old manor houses and removing the noise of their children may have been an early aim. Nevertheless the fetish of privacy was odd in that the landowner and his family hardly escaped from the presence of a considerable staff of live-in servants. For instance, during the seventeenth century men servants were insurance against violence in the countryside, a danger for which Trevor Cliffe states there is 'overwhelming evidence'. The security motive faded in the eighteenth century and even appeals to privacy were supplemented by aesthetic considerations. The purpose of removing buildings was to provide unimpeded views over grassy plains and tastefully arranged clumps of trees. Although the original church might be left isolated in the park when village houses were removed, if the church itself were pulled down a new one was occasionally built, but well away from the big house. An example is the National Trust property of Croome, Worcestershire.

The well-known complaint by some old Roman Catholic writers that after the Reformation the Protestant gentry moved away from the community, up into their parks, is turned on its head by the imparking of recent centuries. Instead of removing themselves, landowners might decide to expel the community instead, remodelling the big house or pulling it down and rebuilding it in whatever was the fashionable style of the day, because the house was likely to occupy a site long before selected as excellent. Between 1710 and 1800, 840 large country houses were built in England, 'dispersed', Horace Walpole said, 'like great rarity plums in a vast pudding of a country'.

Who were the owners? Apart from members of long-standing aristocratic and gentry families, they came from any family that had made money from any conceivable source—court offices, the law, trade, imperial administration and every rising industry, just as they are now joined by foreign investors and English investors who might as well be foreign in that they hide their ownership in tax havens, as well as bankers, hedge-fund managers and entertainers celebrated for the fact of being celebrated. New money at any period, including the present, tends to make a splash with a fashionable house and park in the countryside. Yet the *nouveaux riches* were not the only instruments of upheaval. Old families were perfectly capable of ignoring local feelings and altering the landscape (the Ingilbys, for one, had been at Ripley for centuries). Established owners alert to the currents of agricultural profitability had figured large among the medieval sheep-farmers who expunged so many Midlands villages. When the economy expanded with the growth of trade during the late sixteenth and seventeenth centuries, fresh sources of income emerged, and on the backs of industries transformed in the eighteenth century further waves of new men rode. New entrants deriving their money from particular sources reflected the sequence of development and the larger trends in the economy. When old families died out or landed proprietors went down in agricultural depressions, there were always fresh ones waiting in the wings to establish themselves, build and furnish great mansions, take up country sports and cover their families with rural gentility.

Not every non-agricultural fortune flowed into land but from the earliest days of industrialisation it was the vogue. The cotton spinner, Sir Richard Arkwright, having made a great fortune, bought estates for his sons in various counties. As we noted, his son, likewise Richard, had no difficulty in entering the landed society in Herefordshire and his grandson encouraged a cotton manufacturing friend to buy an estate in that county too. The size of the Arkwright fortune has been said to have been eclipsed by that of the textile merchant, James Morrison, but this is misleading. There was a generation between them—and at a time of rapid economic expansion a generation made a difference. Sir Richard Arkwright died in 1792 whereas Morrison did not become a senior business partner until 1826. Like Arkwright, but later, Morrison was also to acquire a portfolio of estates and place his sons in them; he even bought Beckford's Fonthill. Thus wherever a family fortune had been amassed, it was a common English tendency to lay it out on an estate.

The subsequent fortunes of landownership were not as promising for every family as these examples may imply. During the late nineteenth-century depression, many families quit their estates: in Wiltshire almost all the gentry went under and the chief survivors were a handful of very large proprietors with outside sources of income. Even some of the grandest estates were deeply indebted, with standing timber the only readily saleable asset, so that the financial health of the estate system was to some extent a façade. Investigations of levels of debt have been inconclusive but local studies note that the attractions of a life on the land encouraged over-optimistic investment, especially when product prices were high.

Many heirs of the remaining old families became young officers who were killed in the First World War, and it was afterwards observed that the predominant strain among the gentry no longer had deep roots in the land. As A. G. Macdonnell observed in *England, their England* (1933), the gentry then in possession were only one remove from London's suburbs, Clyde's banks, Boston or India. They were a self-referring, would-be caste, fixated on games of all types rather than merely the customary hunting and shooting. They treated their properties as dormitories and were remarkably unfamiliar with the countryside around them, settling unconcernedly into a landscape where farming was in the doldrums. The new squires played their games and flirted with one another's wives on their lawns almost oblivious to agricultural decay, for farm rents were not the source of their wealth. Demolishing properties that spoiled their view was no longer tempting because they could buy estates with rustic backdrops constructed by their forerunners.

Macdonnell's wave of interwar incomers in turn received a setback during the Second World War from the loss of a new generation of heirs, the damage of military occupation and the imposition of high taxes. Country houses stood abandoned and in the mid-1950s were being demolished at the rate of one per week. *No Voice from the Hall* is the title of John Harris's elegant epitaph for them. It is loss that has entered popular consciousness yet in reality there has been a vigorous recovery, with new incomers and a scarcely acknowledged wave of new construction. Many estates now differ from historical norms, however, in being less often great agricultural enterprises and more often stand-alone show pieces. This is because so many farms and cottages were sold to sitting tenants in the 1920s and again in the 1950s, for example when the Duke of Rutland sold 13,300 acres of his Belvoir estate in 1920 the sale included seven entire villages. Typical country houses no longer tend to be ringed by farms tributary to them or villages that depend on them. They are 'cut flowers' unsustained by the soil; their owners possess their own large dwellings but have no villages to sell or demolish.

But the divestment of landed properties can be exaggerated and the loss of country houses certainly can. Adrian Tinniswood calculates that, although a dozen were lost in Leicestershire between the wars, 95 survive, and although 20 went in Lancashire nearly 200 survive. The only significant village removals in modern times have been by public authorities who in the 1960s bulldozed declining colliery villages in County Durham and shunted the inhabitants into new towns like Peterlee. Even so only three villages in Durham were wholly pulled down, although there were many partial removals. In the history of England as a whole village demolitions had been a far commoner feature.

SOURCES AND FURTHER READING

Albery, A. (2000). Rural depopulation in Sherborne St. John: The nineteenth century. *The Hampshire Family Historian*, 15–16.

Beresford, M. W. (1971). *History on the ground*. London: Methuen.

Beresford, M. W. (1987). *The lost villages of England*. Alan Sutton: Gloucester.

Cobbett, W. (1912). *Rural rides*. London: J. M. Dent & Sons.

Darby, H. C. (Ed.). (1973). *A new historical geography of England*. Cambridge: Cambridge University Press.

Finberg, H. P. R. (Ed.). (1957). *Gloucestershire studies*. Leicester: Leicester University Press.

Harris, J. (1998). *No voice from the hall*. London: John Murray.

Loach, J. (1986). *Parliament and the crown in the reign of Mary Tudor*. Oxford: Oxford University Press.

Macdonnell, A. G. (1949). *England, their England*. London: Macmillan.

Nicolson, A. (2008). *Earls of paradise: England and the dream of perfection*. London: HarperPress.

Prince, H. C. (1967). *Parks in England*. Pinhorns: Shalfleet.

Taylor, C. (1983). *Village and farmstead*. London: George Philip.

Tinniswood, A. (2016). *The long weekend: Life in the English country house between the wars*. London: Jonathan Cape.

Varley, M. (2000, February). The lands that time forgot. *Geographical Magazine*, pp. 27–31.

Wilson, R., & Mackley, A. (2000). *Creating paradise: The building of the English country house 1660–1880*. London: Continuum-3 PL.

Woodward, F. (1983). *Oxfordshire parks*. Woodstock: Oxfordshire Museum Services.

CHAPTER 5

Road Capture

Abstract The closure or diversion of public roads and particularly footpaths was extremely common, yet is almost never mentioned in the secondary literature. It reveals the historical importance to the landed gentry of amenity values, which extended to keeping traffic out of sight. Privatisation is ancient and, although most frequent in the eighteenth and nineteenth centuries, continues to this day with respect to paths. The usual motive was privacy, a consumption good which accordingly demonstrates—contrary to assumptions in economics—that moving public assets into private hands does not mean they will be more efficiently employed. Documentary evidence, though often abundant, is however local or sometimes absent and has to be supplemented or replaced by ground observation.

Keywords Consumption goods • Footpaths • Privatisation of rights-of-way • Public assets • Road capture

The appropriation of rights-of-way, where a landowner forces a change in a route without concern for other users—road capture—is a perpetual but surprisingly overlooked aspect of England's much-studied landscape. There were always more closures and far more diversions of roads than demolitions of villages. There were infinitely more closures of paths. Roads

© The Author(s) 2018

E. L. Jones, *Landed Estates and Rural Inequality in English History*,
Palgrave Studies in Economic History,
https://doi.org/10.1007/978-3-319-74869-6_5

and footpaths were easier marks than villages; this chapter records many instances of both. Modern landowners can still exert power and influence in perpetuating the centuries-old tradition of having rights-of-way altered to suit their whim, though at the present day they tend to target footpaths rather than established roadways. Historically, an existing route could be incorporated within the offending owner's park with minimal effective resistance. Trevor Cliffe tells us that at Methley, Yorkshire, Sir Henry Savile made a new park in 1627 and would not countenance, 'a common road way through it to the markett or anie place else with Carte and Carrage', so that he 'caused the way to be put down'. As a result 'men began to go the newe way in Anno dom 1628'. They had no choice. At Arley, Cheshire, Sir Peter Warburton acquired some of the local roads by virtue of offering to maintain them. He prevented outsiders from using them. Anyone who was caught had to acknowledge in writing that he had 'flitted' his goods through the Arley lanes, which acted as a deterrent.

The fact of road capture, let alone the significance, has very rarely been recognised, Maurice Beresford being almost alone among national scholars in commenting. Yet it should be obvious on the ground: 'regular users of the A350 between Blandford and Shaftesbury are routinely confounded', states a modern article about the old squire, Peter Beckford, 'by a series of hazardous left and right hand bends just north of Stourpaine and some way south of Iwerne Minster'. Though exceptional in the inconvenience and hazard caused to traffic, this is only one of innumerable examples.

The first feature to be noticed is thus the distorted alignment of roads encountered when driving. What draws the eye is typically a large pair of gates where an abrupt right-angled bend turns the road away from a park. Once the road went straight on. The long, intricate history of roads means there are other reasons for sharp bends but being pushed off course by a park boundary is a common one. Although many instances can be confirmed from documents, most of those from early centuries were probably not recorded. The examples that are met with in documents, including the schedules of highway diversions held in county record offices, may however be expanded or supplemented by looking on the map for roads bent around parks.

The evidence for the shifting of roads is both profuse and diffuse. Plenty of cases can be found but no complete gazetteer. My own investigations have found numerous historical road captures and blocked or diverted footpaths in Gloucestershire, Oxfordshire, Wiltshire, Berkshire, Hampshire, Dorset, Devon and Somerset and a scatter of others as distant as Cheshire and Cambridgeshire. A complication is that roads have been realigned as a result of diverse events and various forces, including attempts by public bodies to improve safety or the flow of traffic, and it cannot be assumed that every change was carried out by individual landowners acting selfishly. Given that—for all the instances – we do not know what the universe of evidence really is, we do not know how best to sample it. Proxy efforts at computation might be made but would depend on arbitrary assumptions and be matters of convenience rather than history.

The number of recognisable cases nevertheless remains very large. It can be stated without reserve that the privatisation of public rights-of-way was not unusual, not confined to any given century, and that it continues at the present day—despite the fact that footpaths are supposed to be registered and protected. In 2015, Lord Dyson, Master of the Rolls, gave judgement in the Court of Appeals that two bridleways laid out at Crudwell in Wiltshire according to an enclosure Act of 1801 are still legal rights-of-way. Wiltshire County Council had however refused to put the two on the 'definitive' map and a government inspector had upheld its refusal. Lord Dyson stated that between 500 and 1000 other paths are affected, a broad bracket showing just how limited knowledge is and how inadequate is the protection of public rights-of-way. Worse, any historic footpaths not officially recorded as public by 2026 will be extinguished. Safeguarding them is mainly left to the chance initiative of local people, playing into the hands of those who own land.

Despite seeming of merely local significance, road- and footpath-capture hold interest beyond the topographical. First, they cast into question the economist's a priori assumption that the transfer of communal resources into the hands of an individual means they will be put to more productive use. Greater amenity for a single family does not fall under that head. Even if a proprietor's position were not absolute, he could be sure that the law was on his side or at least that his fellow magistrates would go along with him. After the Highways Act of 1773 a mere two justices of the peace need certify that a proposed alteration of a route was in the public interest; this they were usually willing to do even when the public was blatantly injured.

Admittedly disputes among the elite might frustrate an individual's intentions but this was rare: shifting a road to run outside a park scarcely impinged on neighbouring proprietors and the quid pro quo of support for plans of their own would be a sufficient inducement to them. Only close to towns, whose merchants stood to lose from a road diversion, was there much likelihood of opposition. At Faringdon (Berkshire, now Oxfordshire), the road from Lechlade was moved outside the park of Faringdon House. Ever since then, traffic has been obliged to mount a gradient, a matter of some concern in the days of carts and waggons drawn by horses. On the far side of Faringdon, where another landowner (a *nouveau riche* London chemist) had pushed the Burford road further out, local businessmen went so far as to obtain an Act of parliament moving it back to a gentler slope.

The central aims of road capture, often frankly stated, were akin to those for moving buildings and whole villages: to increase privacy for estate owners, embellish their grounds and ensure an unimpeded view by means of moving pedestrians and traffic out of sight of their dwellings. Despite an overlap in motives from period to period, the impression is that medieval demolitions tended to be to facilitate certain types of farming, early modern ones to secure household privacy, and later ones to acquire uninterrupted views. The urge for joint privacy and aesthetics may be seen in the astonishingly candid report by Humphrey Repton, who stated in his *Fragments on the Theory and Practice of Landscape Gardening* (1816) that he had appropriated twenty-five yards of common land and added it to his own garden. This gave 'a frame to my landscape'. Planting the additional land stopped the poor coming close and peering in, because when a view 'looks as if it belonged to another' it 'robs the mind of the pleasure derived from appropriation'.

Repton did not feel easy with his own behaviour but felt the attraction keenly: 'I have too frequently witnessed a greater satisfaction in turning a public road, in stopping a foot-path, or in hiding a view by a pale and a screen, than in the most beautiful improvements to the scenery.' He found a few landed proprietors who still enjoyed watching the passing show but most disliked the public and increasingly blocked them from view. Fashion had moved on. 'Near London… the views from public roads are all injured by the pales and belts of private property.' The behaviour was as selfish as it was frequent; it was like that described by Dacher Keltner in *The Power Paradox,* previously mentioned.

When did privacy come to matter so much? Fashions change and individuals vary in their willingness to tolerate other people nearby. It usually helps if these others are only servants, who in the last resort do not count and can be ignored. But privacy usually matters a lot, being a type of consumption good. The point is that estates are almost but not quite 'positional goods' whose attraction lies in excluding others; attaining them is a zero-sum game, meaning that what one person holds others cannot have. In societies with an unequal distribution of wealth and income the fate of most people is to be excluded.

Road capture continued down the centuries. For example, the door on the south side of the church at Northmoor, near Oxford, is blocked up and the main entrance is now on the north, the 'devil's side'. This was connected with diverting the road to the north of the church, out of sight of the adjacent farmhouse. It seems to have happened in the sixteenth or seventeenth century, which makes discovering the original event unlikely. At Morville, Shropshire, what had been a dense network of roads, paths and tracks until the late seventeenth century was cleared away, together with the houses around the church, in order to improve the view from the big house. In Gloucestershire, Henry Hicks had a public footpath diverted in 1802, 'indicating a wish to remain a clothier aloof and isolated on his estate'. Demands for privacy were not always satisfied at first but further bites of the cherry were taken, as at Stoke Poges, Buckinghamshire, where a lane was steered away from a gentrified seventeenth-century farmhouse in 1812, a second diversion in 1832 created a right-angled bend in the road which is still there, and a third diversion occurred in 1925. In the early twenty-first century, advertisements for expensive properties in the *Financial Times* continue to offer the drawcard of 'no public access'.

Keeping the public at arm's length was the purpose of physically removing and rebuilding whole villages. Milton Abbas, Dorset, is a well-known example, carried out despite a Quaker lawyer delaying removal by refusing to cede his property (even though part of it was spitefully flooded). For Victorian and later landowners the prevention of disturbance to game became an urgent purpose. On the Hampshire-Berkshire border, a bridge over the river Enborne was opened in the 1990s to re-establish the right of crossing, the original bridge having been blown up by a landowner who claimed that public access interrupted his duck shoot.

Privacy was oddly selective, given that country houses, even farms, were full of folk, crammed with servants. Privacy was concealed in plain sight by a stylised behaviour that Westerners might think odd if they encountered it among the Japanese. In many households servants were only partly in evidence as they went about their chores. Backstairs helped to keep them out of sight. The effect was to secure the semblance of privacy by pretending that one's own staff did not exist. Passers-by were not so readily dismissed. Distance from them and the demand for an uninterrupted prospect surfaced (though that is scarcely the word) at Westonbirt, Gloucestershire, where the passing road was sunk into the ground in order that traffic should not sully the view, or alternatively at Wheatfield, Oxfordshire, where an embankment was raised to conceal the public road from the great house's sight. The taste for privacy and uninterrupted scenery seems to have increased over time: when the Ashford to Canterbury road in Kent was diverted to enclose a paddock in 1726, a gazebo was built expressly to view the traffic, but in 1780 Lord Barrington, descendant of Roundheads, did away with his gazebo at Shrivenham, Berkshire (now Oxfordshire). Hitherto, ladies of his household used to sit in it to see the carriages go by, but now Barrington shifted the road to run outside his park. Refuge from strangers had become fashionable and more prized than watching the passing show.

What artificial landscape modification represented was conspicuous consumption, including a desire for amenity widely construed. In the long term, private amenity values—the furnishing of mansions and setting out of pleasure grounds—were irrelevant to the mass of society or were incidental, like the employment of economically unproductive servants. In the course of remodelling, adjacent farmland was not infrequently reassigned for leisure. Admittedly eighteenth-century parks were grazed by prize cattle or sheep but this was lawn-mowing before the nineteenth-century invention of the mower. It was seldom serious livestock husbandry. Once the ancient aim of enclosing land for deer parks had faded, the purposes of imparking were ornamentation and preserving seclusion. The opportunity cost of devoting resources to these ends was not negligible. When the second Earl of Nottingham built a new house in Rutland between 1694 and 1702 he found the park too small and so incorporated additional farmland, losing, as Maurice Beresford says, £600 per year in rents 'as the price of his satisfied eye'.

There was some chronological clustering of privatisations, pointing to specific influences. One was the Highways Act of 1773. The previous lack of such an Act had barely deterred alterations but the 1773 Act simplified procedures and reduced the chances of a challenge to road alterations. In Victorian times, proposals for extinguishing or altering footpaths were regularised in a fashion reminiscent of the posting of banns for marriage; notices were printed in local newspapers and posted for four successive Sundays at either end of the affected stretch, as well as on the church door. A grace period followed and meetings of the vestry were held. It was all legal or rather legalistic, for few would dare to object. In the 1930s, Lord Rothermere secured agreement to closing a path in Wychwood but those who attended the 'public' meetings were merely his own tenants.

A face-saving distinction is often made between old money, said to have been relatively tolerant, and rich incomers, such as Rothermere, who were determined to assert their power over rural society. Some proprietors may have been willing to curb the excesses of their estate stewards, who had a little brief authority and could not be relied on to be charitable, but absentee landlords typically delegated the management of their land. Edward Fitzgerald, writing of the area about Woodbridge, Suffolk, condemned the 'petty race of Squires', who had replaced earlier owners and were busy stopping up footpaths, for 'only [using] the Earth for an Investment'. M. K. Ashby contrasted the towering stiles put up by newcomers at Bledington, Gloucestershire, with the manageable ones of old-established landowners, but while the difference is plausible there seems to be no general analysis distinguishing behaviour in the two groups. Large farmers could be just as prone as landowners to ride roughshod over public rights. *British History Online* notes that the inhabitants of Pyrton, Oxfordshire, suffered when the footpath to the next settlement was closed at the behest of farmers who claimed its mere existence would encourage trespassers.

Disorderly objections to the usurping of rights-of-way were most likely in towns and cities. Apart from the urban mob, someone from the middle classes might call 'foul', as when a local brewer challenged the Royal Ranger in court in 1758 and confirmed a right-of-way across Richmond Park which had been walled in by Charles I. Even so the law of access remained one sided, provoking a letter from Octavia Hill in *The Times* of 14 September, 1892, complaining of legal bias in favour of landowners. Near London there was an effort in the late nineteenth century to counter the closing of commons and diverting of footpaths, the Commons Preservation Society being especially forceful on the North Downs. But in the countryside there were few Village Hampdens, the lawyer at Milton Abbas having been a shining exception. Where villages were owned outright by the local squire, challenging him, even if one could afford the legal fees, raised the threat of losing one's cottage and job. The circumstances were akin to the enclosure movement, where resistance from below jeopardised one's chance of employment on the new ring-fenced farms. Nevertheless, gatherings to protest against closing footpaths, which was an immediate affront, may have been more frequent than any against enclosure.

Enclosure was a great tidying process, accompanied by transferring resources into the hands of the larger landholders. A landscape laid out in tenant farms made it easier to introduce new crops and rotations not readily compatible with common field routines. The motive is chiefly described as raising agricultural productivity but often this is speculation; the analogy of the privatisation of public roads suggests that such an outcome was uncertain. Estate owners stood to gain the lion's share of the land regardless of whether or not they introduced husbandry improvements, which no one obliged them to do and which they may have delayed. Road capture, on the other hand, did not display enclosure's ambiguity between productivity and acquisition. There was no question of efficiency gains and the effect was usually the opposite. It was a sign of how little concern for the public was shown by landowners down the ages. As the modern editor of Pevsner's *Oxfordshire* points out, the landed class had no social conscience.

The diversion of roads occurred chiefly in the period 1660–1880, although indeterminate examples may come from earlier periods, some medieval instances being known. The later regularisation of legal procedures and consequent recording of requests must bias the chronology towards the present, just as concentrating on the history of turnpikes (because they generated formal evidence) skews the chronology of road communications. Nevertheless parish historians can be found who have noticed distortions of the road network and the elimination of footpaths, and followed them up in the records. By the nineteenth century, public outcries and even the throwing down of gates were being reported in provincial newspapers. But most captures, especially of footpaths and especially in earlier centuries, are not easily traced. Study is complicated because districts varied in their original densities of rights-of-way.

Given the enormous area of the country occupied by estates, the opportunity for meddling with rights-of-way was immense. What, then, was the scale of road capture and what were the costs? No reasonable means exist to compute either magnitude. Yet because the total number of closures and diversions was very large, the loss of travellers' time, though small at individual sites, was surely large in aggregate. It is easy to overlook individually minor and widely dispersed changes. Contrary to standard histories, which incline to celebrate all developments in transport and communications as progressive, the procedure was economically and socially negative. It was rent-seeking behaviour, like so much activity by landowners, part of the market failure that arose from the concentration of property ownership. Moreover, it was essentially permanent: the road system is still wriggly and, now that roads have been sealed, is rarely straightened. The sharp bends are fossilised and continue to produce vehicle accidents. Reports in local newspapers make this plain, although there seems no single source that gathers together the precise locations and circumstances of road accidents. The rolling English road was not made by the rolling English drunkard; it is the legacy of generations of selfish landowners. The proprietors of estates do not suggest restoring the original routes and, if they did, county councils would not thank them for the extra road-making expense.

Historically, roads that ran hard by big houses on country estates were prime targets for elimination. Footpaths were, if anything, still more vulnerable. Where it was desired to allow passage by workers to grounds, farms or church, yet still to channel their access, former roads might be retained as footpaths. Maps and the ground make this plain: roads end or turn away at the edge of estates, continuing (if at all) across the park only as paths, which is therefore a pointer to past road capture. At Compton Chamberlayne, Wiltshire, the Penruddocks revamped the system of routes in the late eighteenth and nineteenth centuries and bent the road around the edge of their park. This is a little hint that, had the Penruddock Rising against Cromwell succeeded in 1655, there might have been no great social benefit. Royalist rebels were really concerned to re-establish their own positions.

The overall network of footpaths has been eroded for centuries and attrition continues today, with the connivance of the highway departments of county councils. Recently it was ordained that a path should be moved to 'a respectful distance' from a house of moderate note in Gloucestershire, a privilege not granted to ordinary taxpayers. Individuals in the public eye, such as actors and footballers, petition for diversions away from their houses on the grounds that they may be stalked—but the existence of a right-of-way should have been plain when they bought their properties and in any case there are laws against stalking. The leading non-governmental organisation (NGO) self-appointed to represent the walking public, the Ramblers, may offer an objection but seems not to concern itself with minor alterations and fails to take notice of the way long-standing opportunities for approaching historic buildings and other features are eliminated. The body may have become a prisoner of regulatory capture.

Assertions that footpaths are inherently unnecessary or vexatious go back a long way. Referring to a closure at Wilton, the gardener, J. C. Loudon, wrote in 1834 that 'the inhabitants are quite aware of the injustice which has been done them in excluding them from their ancient rights of walking by the side of the river in the park; but so powerful is a wealthy family in a small country place, that neither the corporation of Wilton united, nor any individual among them, would incur the risk of reclaiming public right'. The park here was the one where the village of Washern had been demolished. The majority of captures have proved irreversible, though there is an occasional piquant exception: for instance at Minal, also in Wiltshire, a farmer made his senior man a constable and in 1827 secured the citizen's arrest of a shopkeeper who was driving his waggon along a track. Although the route had been used for decades, the shopkeeper received a heavy fine and the farmer obtained a stopping order. Yet in 1982 a Department of the Environment report confirmed the same track as a bridleway.

The usual claim of those who dismiss the case for public footpaths is that they have become redundant. Their purpose, it is claimed, was to enable farmhands to get to their work but today, when farms employ few hands, they are no longer needed. This misuses history. The earlier network of paths is only discoverable where pre-enclosure maps are available and it is this that has been cut to pieces, often into lengths that are hard to use because they do not knit together. Certainly paths were used to get to work but this is to mistake the original situation. Before the nineteenth century large stretches of the landscape lay open. They were less subject to intransigent assertions of private ownership. Rural populations were smaller and the almost industrial rearing of gamebirds to be shot had scarcely begun. The crossing of vast tracts of the countryside was less hindered – a more rural population knew to steer clear of livestock and not to trample the crops. In his *Rural Rides* of the 1820s, William Cobbett mentions heading out across open downs in an approximate direction, relying on shepherds to correct his course. Cobbett left more of a record than most travellers yet was merely one of many who set out like that.

What happened afterwards was confinement and privatisation, which narrowed the broad routes where it had formerly been possible to zigzag around muddy patches and other obstacles. Today the intensive use of footpaths near settlements can render them almost impassable in winter. In the past they were meant to stay separate from horse roads in order to safeguard pedestrians from trampled mud in wet weather. Hedges were not expected to hide paths from wind and sun and hinder them from drying out, as happened with plantings after enclosure. The subsequent narrowing has not been reversed—paths have not been widened to meet modern densities of use. The crux is that they represent the remnants of what was once freer access to the countryside; they are not the needless residue of networks established purely for workaday convenience. From freedom to wander, access has retreated, shrinking considerably in parishes reorganised by parliamentary enclosure and shrinking again through repeated privatisations. The enclosure of 1812 at Shipston-on-Stour, Warwickshire, stopped up every footpath in the parish, any from the outside being blocked just inside the parish boundary and diverted sharply to the nearest road. Paths were run along the sides of the new roads, however awkward this was.

Parliamentary enclosure did not affect the whole country. It is therefore an exaggeration to say that the minor road system is entirely its legacy but it had an impact where it did take place. The Earl of Coventry requested the enclosure commissioners for Chipping Campden to allow him a driveway for the use of his family and Lord Northwick so that, as the author of a local history remarks, 'ordinary folk had to take the long way round'. When he bought a wood on the Chilterns, Richard Mabey found that the enclosure of 1853 had stopped up thirteen old roads and footpaths. Another formal process, the establishment of turnpikes, had similar consequences. Nearby routes—'shunpikes' – that might be used to avoid paying tolls tended to be blocked.

Between the wars landowners were asked which paths they accepted as running across their properties, inviting another curtailing of the system. Where Rural District Councils were largely comprised of farmers a minimum of paths was dedicated to public use and it is said that at least as late as 2005 Wiltshire had never prosecuted a single closure. It must be admitted that reductions can occur on the demand as well as the supply side: the introduction of bicycles at the end of the nineteenth century led farmworkers to abandon some footpaths in favour of the high road. This could happen fast. A woman who returned about 1900 to Sherridge, Worcestershire, after three years in Japan was struck by the disappearance of the field paths, which she attributed to the adoption of bicycles with pneumatic tyres. The path network shrank where local people ceased to be concerned about it. Those who still worked on the farms were disinclined to irritate their employers. Footpaths became a leisure resource. Even disregarding legality and fairness, the growth of an increasingly sedentary urban population using footpaths for purposes of health and recreation means their importance has been revived. They are however imprisoned within the straitjacket of past restrictions.

Among the attritions of footpaths, some were closed by individuals who might have been expected to be more public-spirited: Cobbett closed a path; William Morris did so too; the Chief Constable of Wiltshire wired up a path near his home at West Lavington, although a local cut the wire; and Wedgwood Benn's family stand accused of sharing 'the aristocratic penchant for keeping oiks off their land: the sea wall at the edge of the [Essex] farm has long been off limits to ramblers'. When it was pointed out that a Countryside Commission survey found 6000 miles of blocked footpaths in England, the fact was not contested by the Chairman of the Country Landowners Association, nor did he deny that he had blocked one himself, though he put the blame on his tractor driver.

Beleaguered as the network is, the survival of so many paths is almost surprising. Not that it is impossible to find acts of resistance at any period, for instance riots at Ogley, Staffordshire, in 1838 when access to the common was stopped up. Resistance was most likely to succeed where urban populations were involved, though not all towns were effective in protecting their assets: even fashionable Cecily Hill in Cirencester 'was eventually robbed of its path out of the town to Minchinhampton and Bisley by the formation of the [Bathursts'] Park and the building of new Stroud Road'. One example of footpath 'turnings' attributed successful resistance in 1836 against what were termed the 'Windsor-footpath-stopping-surveyors' to a friendly society called the 'Society of Good Intent'. When in 1852 the Great Northern Railway Company diverted footpaths at Hornsey, London, and built across one of them, removing the parish's boundary stones in the process, the vestry obliged it to restore several paths.

In 1883, one of the Sackvilles blocked the bridleway across his park at Knole, Kent. He was unlucky in that the growing population of Sevenoaks had become accustomed to walking there. One thousand people came and the posts were broken. The next night, led by a solicitor's clerk and with one-third of the Kent constabulary in attendance, they paraded through the entrance. Sackville won an action for trespass in the High Court. He retreated, however, and permitted pedestrians to use the path. In 1897, Sir William Rose blocked footpaths near Farnham, Surrey, but over one hundred people gathered, overwhelmed the former Metropolitan policemen he had hired and restored access: this was known as 'The Battle of Moor Park'. Another interesting case took place at Little Gaddesden, Hertfordshire, in 1927. On the break-up of the Ashridge estate, one of the big farms was sold and immediately came out in a rash of notice boards, blocked footpaths and locked and barred roadways. This had long been a squire's village and most of the inhabitants were unwilling to express more than covert opposition. The only people who went out to pull down the fences were the schoolmaster, the churchwarden, the rector's son, a well-known poet and a handful of others. The churchwarden asked the school-master to search the parish papers, where he was extraordinarily lucky to find a seventeenth-century deed stating that Church Road was 'to be and to remayne a comon high way for ever'. At that point the diocesan solici-tor came and in his presence the locked gate was broken open. Other examples of resistance did occur, usually produced by similar coalitions of residents, dissident members of the landed class and professional people. An episode from between the wars was portrayed by John Moore in *Brensham Village*.

The intimidation of users of rights-of-way continues. In 2010 the for-mer vice-chairman of a stockbroking firm had his gamekeepers harry peo-ple off old paths in Kent, brazenly asserting that there were quite enough footpaths for the needs of the community. The effrontery of assaults on the common weal knows few bounds. A query to the *Shooting Times* (6 November, 2013) asked how to deal with people who insist on using pub-lic footpaths that run through a shoot. The answer was that the onus is on the guns to ensure the safety of users, which may mean stopping the shoot until the walker is clear – it was assumed no walker would exercise his or her legal right to linger on the path. A twenty-first century incident occurred when the public school, Harrow, gated a nineteenth-century footpath through its 400-acre site. It constructed sports' pitches across a right-of-way. The matter was contested. Among documents on the Internet is a counsel's surely tendentious opinion in favour of what is for-mally 'the Free Grammar School of John Lyon ("the School")'. Maurice Beresford came on a public footpath traversing a garden and lawn to which the owners had objected. Their solicitor's searches had failed to discover the existence of a path which had been there before 1596!

Seventy or eighty footpath diversions are applied for nationally every week, most unopposed. In 1987, when a walker had only a one-in-three chance of completing a two-mile stretch unimpeded, the (then) Countryside Commission proposed to open 140,000 miles of paths by 2000, but had already fallen far behind in the early 1990s. Essentially the paths had been blocked or closed. Fences and hedges around the smallest modern gardens reveal an extraordinary demand for privacy among the English. This may be partly imitative but it is tempting to account for it in terms of the scar-city of land in relation to the size of population. Yet factor proportions arguments like that cannot apply to large estates. Ultimately road and path captures appear as side effects of rising wealth. They signal social and eco-nomic success. They also reflect a desire for dominance, as well as for con-spicuous consumption in the guise of the rural amenities sought by the landed pyramid endlessly reproducing itself in English society. Public access to the countryside is far greater in Scotland and Scandinavia, which have different histories.

SOURCES AND FURTHER READING

AN ACT for repairing the road from... Faringdon... to Burford 3 Will.IV, Sess, 1833.

Ashby, M. K. (1974). *The changing English village: A history of Bledington, Gloucestershire in its setting 1066–1914.* Kineton: The Roundhead Press.

Bell, V. (1950). *The Dodo: The story of a village schoolmaster.* London: Faber & Faber.

Belsey, V. (2001). *Discovering green lanes.* Totnes: Green Books.

Castor, H. (2005). *Blood and roses.* London: Faber and Faber.

Cliffe, J. T. (1999). *The world of the country house in seventeenth-century England.* New Haven: Yale University Press.

Dorset Ancestors. dorset-ancestors.com/, 'Peter Beckford – Squire of Steepleton', 24/12/2009.

Loudon, J. C. (1990). *In search of English gardens.* London: Century.

Ramm, D. (2006). *The secrets of countryside access.* No place stated: The East Berks Ramblers.

Sherwood, J., & Pevsner, N. (2002). *Oxfordshire.* New Haven: Yale University Press.

CHAPTER 6

Killing Grounds

Abstract A further neglected aspect of amenity considerations shaping rural society and the economy was blood sports. This involved the ritual or at least stylised killing of birds and animals, the latent function being male bonding among the elite. Blood sports were ancient pastimes of those with access to land but were formalised by the Victorians. A side-effect was the protection of the preferred prey by severe Game Laws that came to dominate rural society. A wide range of quarry narrowed towards the fox and pheasant, whose hunting and shooting became obsessions of the rich and led to extraordinary slaughter. The importance of the activity is signalled by the fact that during periods of agricultural depression shooting rights often became more valuable than farm rents.

Keywords Blood sports • Fox-hunting • Game Laws • Pheasant shooting • Shooting rights

In 1655, the Penruddock conspirators against Cromwell gathered under cover of fox hunting, which the Protector had omitted to ban, although he did forbid horse racing. In itself hunting the fox would not have excited suspicion, although later commentators tended to think that the true gentlemanly sport in those days was deer coursing. They believed that fox hunting became the fashion only after the Interregnum, when deer parks had been broken open by the peasantry and no larger quarry than the fox was readily available. This was plausible and fitted some of the facts, but students of the history of sport have since painted a more varied picture.

Throughout history the ritual killing of animals had been kept as exclusive to powerful people and as formal in procedure as possible. Vast drives were held by the ancient rulers of Central Asia and also took place until the recent past in Central and Eastern Europe. Immense bags and ease of despatching the quarry were what flunkies and local hosts strove to ensure. Much ceremony attached to deer hunting. In England the quarry, alive or dead, was always a suitable gift for the rich and influential. During the reign of Elizabeth I, fresh carcasses of deer were still being presented to the canons of St Paul's Cathedral under a thirteenth-century bequest. The canons paraded in sacred vestments and the bucks were carried in procession with garlands on their heads. The attractiveness and significance of chasing and killing deer were likewise revealed by the elaborate hunting lodges built for royalty, King John for instance, and for other prominent people who wished to offer spectators a grand show. The National Trust owns a lodge at Sherborne, Gloucestershire, where John Dutton obtained a licence from Oliver Cromwell to import deer from Wychwood Forest. Dogs chasing the deer could be watched from the roof. The veneration in which deer hunting was held was also symbolised by the dedication of chapels to St Hubert, patron saint of hunters.

Changes in the types of sports were seldom abrupt and what happened to deer hunting is obscured by poor recording, overlaps among various sports, and poorly discerned differences in preference between one period and the next. Under the Commonwealth, falconry was curtailed as a pleasure thought too closely associated with the monarchy. Charles II restored its popularity but was the last king to fly his own hawks, since for obscure reasons hawking was already falling out of fashion and was to survive only as a niche pastime. During and indeed long before the seventeenth century, deer hunting may have attracted the greatest prestige but in reality ordinary country gentlemen had been promiscuous in their habits, coursing deer, coursing hares, hunting foxes (some were preserved for the purpose since as early as Elizabethan times), going on rough shoots, angling when it suited them and meeting at popular bowling greens. No single activity had yet become a general craze and only later did sports become stylised and ranked in esteem. Until that came about men chose their fancy in the morning and hunted by whatever means came to hand.

The upper classes once saw riding and shooting (with bow or gun) as a preparation for war or for self-defence in a countryside where violent conflicts might erupt among neighbours. As late as the start of the Second World War, the yeomanry took their horses to France, futile though cavalry were in the face of mechanised warfare. Finally it dawned on them that they must switch to tanks. Riding had outlived any martial purpose, and only leisure and social display persisted as reasons why the man on horseback remained astride. The countryside was a stage to strut on but only for play-acting.

The landed class's social inferiors saw two merits in killing wildlife beyond enjoying the chase: filling the cooking pot and suppressing pests that preyed on crops and livestock. Villagers concerned for their chicken arranged communal hunts for foxes, using nets because they were the most effective tool. There were sporting and convivial elements to what they did but the main purpose was pragmatic. They did not enact formal rules or bag limits to increase the effort that had to be made; those were the artificial devices of rich men trying to prolong their elaborate games.

Ordinary villagers were not alone, however, in finding utilitarian reasons for slaughtering animals: the gentry may have had martial schemes at the back of their minds and sport at the front, but they were not oblivious to culinary purpose. In the seventeenth and eighteenth centuries they hunted for the table and became jealous of the wildlife—deer, hares, rabbits, pheasants, partridges and fish—on and around their property, because they wanted a regular supply for themselves. Raw meat did not keep well and if preserved by smoking or salting was less palatable than when it was fresh. What brought a measure of change was a fairly simple technology available to those who had enough land: the icehouse, which kept meat cool for long periods and was widely adopted during the eighteenth century. A century later there was another step up in the availability of wild food when game and wildfowl were brought from greater and greater distances. English markets became filled with duck taken in the decoy traps of Holland, carried by ship and distributed via the rail network.

None of these developments stemmed hunting in England but they increasingly swung its balance towards the hobbyist element. The mid-eighteenth century saw a soaring growth in riding to hounds after foxes, representing a major stage in the formalisation of blood sports. Since foxes are inedible the most that could be claimed was that fox hunting was a form of pest control, though that was a self-serving rationalisation given that organised hunts were inefficient replacements for the practice of netting. The uniformed and stylised hunt created an unbridgeable social divide between the people on horseback and followers on foot. Social harmony was not improved by the enclosures and the ploughing of commons and heaths in the eighteenth century, because although the convention was that the hunt could be followed anywhere, agricultural improvement shrank the area well suited for it. Local lords commandeered much of what rough land was left by the enclosures and everyone else had to make what shift they could.

The claims of landowners went well beyond the demands of the pot, so that from the eighteenth century blood sports became ends in themselves. They became crazes. Complete information has not survived but there is far, far more than enough to demonstrate what might be called the sporting turn. It has been plausibly claimed that estates dedicated to shooting more than doubled in number from 1760 to 1840. Old game books occasionally survive but the main sources are mentions in memoirs and descriptions of rural life, of which there are thousands. They testify to the growing centrality of sport in the life of the gentry and aristocracy. In addition there are endless legal and newspaper records about the Game Laws and the disproportionately severe punishments inflicted on poachers. In the next chapter two illuminating cases involving poachers will be described in unvarnished detail.

Punishments were imposed by the very men whose property had been assaulted; they sat on the bench to dispense justice in cases where they were personally involved. From the mass of testimony about their harshness, we need cite only a representative example that concerns the overbearing John Benett of Pythouse, Wiltshire. Benett was accused of convicting a poor man and committing him to gaol, where he was loaded with irons, merely for picking up a rabbit which his dog had accidentally killed. More than that, in 1818 Benett and a member of the Penruddock family ordered two married men, each with seven or eight children, to be publicly and severely flogged through the parish for taking home two small bundles of broom after they had been out all night in the depths of winter watching for poachers on Penruddock's land.

Blood sports were central parts of their existence for a majority of the landed class. Lady Mary Wortley Montagu remarked that the residents of eighteenth-century Wiltshire (she meant the landowners) were 'insensible to other pleasures than hunting and drinking'. 'Sport had become the opium of the upper classes', says Peter Mandler, 'indicating some structural defect in the society which over-indulges it'. This goes some way towards explaining the rigour with which they defended the game on their estates. Obsession is scarcely too strong a term for the state of mind that overtook such people. Insofar as the situation altered (the underlying motives did not), the changes mainly concerned shifts in the most fashionable target species. Whereas fox hunting had become an absolute fever among horse riders from the mid-eighteenth century, the mass killing of pheasants in continental-style battues or in drives ensured that shooting was added to the top of the Victorian sporting tree.

Hunting and shooting continued side by side but there was friction between them. Maintaining a population of foxes did not sit comfortably with safeguarding 'chicken runs' full of reared pheasants. Hunt supporters resented any closure of coverts through which they wanted to ride and remained convinced that gamekeepers were guilty of trying to eliminate the fox. On hunting estates, gamekeepers dared not be caught shooting foxes. Most landlords hunted or permitted the local hunt to ride over their land—hence they expected foxes to be 'found' on their property, although they were likely to enjoy shooting too. This faced the keeper with the incompatible task of maximising the populations of both foxes and gamebirds.

When times were good, landlords were prepared to forego some of their agricultural income for the sake of the sports of their choice. Whichever sports were chosen, opportunity costs were imposed on society because resources were diverted from productive uses at times of considerable poverty. When farm rents fell in the late nineteenth century, landowners needed extra-agricultural income and they set about building shooting lodges to let to rich, socially aspiring, Londoners. Even then they tried to attract tenants who hunted as well as shot, for fear that they might otherwise shoot foxes or encourage the keepers to do so.

In Victorian times, excess marked most sports. One has only to read the novels of Surtees to sense how compelling fox hunting had become. Keen hunters tried to maximise the number of days they spent in the saddle. With shooting, the emphasis fell on killing the largest possible number of birds. Certain individuals carried this to extremes and were as closely emulated as other people could manage. The pinnacle of the sporting elite was reached by the Marquis of Ripon who displayed the competitiveness implied by ever larger tallies of dead animals. Until the First World War the annual bag on his estate at Nocton, Lincolnshire, was about 10,000 pheasants, partridges and ducks. After the war the estate was turned into a giant potato farm but still with a shoot, which was served by light rail carrying a train with an enclosed carriage for the guns, waggons for the beaters and a game cart. The carriage, which had originally been designed to carry high-ranking officers to the front during the battle of the Somme, was in use until 1960.

Ripon himself had accounted for over 500,000 head of game before dropping dead on a grouse moor in 1923. Joseph Nickerson (1914–1990), a rich Lincolnshire farmer and plant breeder, shot about half this number but because he was determined to vaunt his own performance he calculated that Ripon's half-a-million head was bulked out with rabbits and hares. Accordingly he matched his own bag strictly of birds over the twenty-four years to 1988 against Ripon's equivalent bag over twenty-four years to 1922. Whereas Ripon had managed a paltry 187,763 birds Nickerson shot 188,172! His *A Shooting Man's Creed* catches the spirit of his type and its selfishness. 'Nothing can be done about rights of way', he moaned, 'except to ensure that ramblers keep to the paths'.

The temptation is to dwell on such picturesque cases, of which there are plenty, but it invites the question of how typical they were. They were unusual but not necessarily exceptional. Michael Bloch reports the incredulity with which the tenth Duke of Beaufort greeted the aesthetes, James and Alvilde Lees-Milne, when they were tenants on his estate at Badminton. 'What is the *point* of those Lees-Milnes?' he asked, 'They don't hunt, they don't shoot, they don't fish.' The Duke dodged serving in the Second World War on health grounds but still hunted an average of four days per week. David Cannadine records in *The Decline and Fall of the British Aristocracy* that Lord Leconfield, out hunting in 1940, came across a crowd watching football and berated them for having nothing better to do in wartime. Testimony in the literature for over two centuries shows that these men were only extreme representatives of a familiar type. Endless data bear out the tendency of sporting activity to absorb the time, attention and resources of the modal landowner during and after Victorian times. Farm management was delegated to agents and bailiffs.

Until the second half of the twentieth century almost anything could be trapped, shot or chased to death by hounds or harriers, just as it could be killed by gamekeepers, collected for stuffing by the taxidermists in every town or squirreled away in private cabinets of birds' eggs and butterflies. Ultimately legislation put some abuses of wildlife out of bounds, chiefly those practised by lower classes already hampered by their lack of access to land. The hobby of small boys who collected birds' eggs was proscribed, though as the late Felicity Palmer pointed out decades ago in a letter to *The Times,* any farmer wishing to amalgamate his fields could set fire with impunity to a dividing hedge full of nests and nestlings. When it was the better-off who found their pastimes curbed – by new laws, too crowded a countryside, or prey that was too tame—their keener members could continue big game hunting in the colonies or after the fall of communism go shooting in Eastern Europe. Present-day advertisements offer better terms overseas than at home: 'no bag limit, you decide when to stop shooting'.

One way to visualise the history of blood sports is to see them as a menu of choices. It is too simple to think of the present as historically given – handed down intact from the ancestors. Although the sporting press strives to imply continuity where there is really imitation, what happens today does not descend automatically from an ever-present set of activities. Some sports have declined while others have maintained their popularity. Current sports had a long history before the Victorians reorganised them but so did others that are no longer practised. The historical or genetic approach does not take into account those that have dropped out of use, like hawking and otter hunting, or illustrate the social forces supporting those that persist. Better to explain the practices in vogue at any one time as choices made by successive generations from the options open to them.

What is on offer, so to speak, is always the product of multiple influences whose content and interaction varies with circumstances. Changing land use acting via the differential availability of habitats has been one factor, yet, while it is tempting to resort to this as the dominant explanation, by itself it never fully determined what was done. This is evident in the case of the transition from deer to fox as the preferred prey; it was not a straightforward response to the pulling down of deer parks under the Commonwealth, since these could be, and sometimes were, re-established. Topography as well as land use also enters into the equation, as with the move of the centre of gravity of pheasant shooting towards the hilly western side of the country during the late nineteenth century, when it was realised that the greater 'available relief' there obliged the birds to fly high and present more interesting shots. Low-lying East Anglia thereafter concentrated on becoming the home of partridge shooting.

Since farm crops underwent significant changes, agriculture also seems a candidate for bringing about alterations in sport. When blood sports were systematised they became ends in themselves but they did not do so untrammelled; few landowners were so rich as utterly to ignore every other consideration. Farmers had to bow before sporting requirements but landlords had to adapt reciprocally to altered methods of farming if they were to go on receiving good rents. Cropping and sport co-evolved and it is hard to discern which led and which followed—a little of both, no doubt, according to period, region, ecosystem, quarry and crop. In the Age of the Pheasant before the First World War, farming on a proportion of the biggest estates took second place to shooting, just as the landscape of some districts had earlier been modified for fox hunting. But this was a luxury best afforded by men who depended least on farm rents. Landlords who relied heavily on rents quit during the arable depression of the late nineteenth century, unless they were able to rent out the sporting rights, which could become more profitable than letting to farmers: 'the partridge', says Horn, 'had been the salvation of Norfolk farming'. The economic importance of blood sports was thus demonstrated.

The sportsmen of the upper elite had always hired some labour but the vast shoots of Victorian times took a decisive turn towards externalising effort. This reflected both the master-man divide in the countryside and the effective industrialisation of rural sport. All the main sports were affected, mutatis mutandis, but shooting above all. It was transformed by improvements in the efficiency of shotguns and cartridges, the use of selected breeds of dogs, the artificial rearing of game and the planting of more coverts and shelter belts. The 'guns' no longer needed to learn the ground in any detail, everything was done for them bar pulling the trigger. Railways fostered their consumerist detachment and facilitated the urban descent on the countryside, already foreshadowed in the early nineteenth century by the annual arrival of fly-fishermen travelling in coaches from London to the trout streams. Motor cars acted as a force-multiplier to the railways.

The gamekeepers who attended on this hyper-organised pursuit were charged with reducing the numbers of predators or competitors with game, such as magpies, crows, stoats and birds of prey of every description. Game Laws had long stigmatised villagers as pests too and sought to exclude them from many hunting practices and away from large, edible or fashionable prey. The rural working classes were finally defeated by enclosure and the failure of the 'last labourers' revolt' in 1830. Their legal participation in blood sports was reduced to the margins, such as a token attendance as foot followers of the fox hunts. They could not afford to ride nor join the shoots, where their presence would not have been welcome; it would not be in fashionable circles today. The television presenter, Adam Henson, used to go beating at Chatsworth for the Duchess of Devonshire and reports that many of her guests would not speak to the beaters and gamekeepers.

Rural working-class attention had been diverted to team games like football on pitches provided by the squires with the effect of luring villagers from the fields and pheasant coverts. The progressive shrinkage of accessible land made restrictions easier to police, though it drove the more recalcitrant or hungriest men to risk poaching in the preserves of landed estates. The densest populations of game species, sources of protein for half-starved families, were to be found there. Game birds were reared and fed like domestic chicken, attracting both wild and human predators. Laws were tightened and were enforced by gamekeepers who tried to deter poachers by setting mantraps, legally until 1828 and surreptitiously much later, as is revealed by an occasional court case. William Cobbett, when in Kent on his *Rural Rides* (4 September, 1823), noted the irony of a sign reading, 'PARADISE PLACE. Spring guns and steel traps are set here'. During the final years of the nineteenth century the standard of living of farmhands did creep up a little and offences against the Game Laws subsided, but even at that late period 18 per cent of all prosecutions in Bedfordshire were tried under their heading.

Nothing divided rural society into haves and have-nots more than the acquisition and appropriation of land and water, together with the animals, birds and fish living there. The privatisation of land by the aristocracy, gentry and clergy, especially in the eighteenth century, is the most familiar element. Exclusion from the rivers is less well known but is equally emblematic of what happened overall. Landed proprietors contrived to acquire fishing rights and exclude ordinary people from the streams where they had fished since ancient times. The environmental historian, Richard Hoffman, has suggested that Britain could in a sense 'afford' the withdrawal of freshwater fisheries into private sporting hands because as an archipelago it could access marine fisheries to replace them. This was a fortunate coincidence.

What purpose lay—and lies – behind the frenetic shooting of game-birds, running down foxes with hounds and hooking fish in the rivers? Modern people see little of it and take it for granted as a traditional feature of English life. Only the converted could really approve, however, of the slaughtering or maiming of wildlife. The Dutch anthropologist, Heidi Dahles, who wrote a book about shooting in the Netherlands, concluded that 'hunting [shooting] cannot be understood in terms of instrumental behaviour. When all the rational arguments in support of hunting have been adduced, its expressive functions remain the only convincing ones. Hunting indicates social status and serves male identity functions.' Male bonding—extended into business dealings, especially on the grouse moor—and the affirmation of status through privileged access to land and water are what lie behind the activity. The royals have always inclined to set the social and sporting tone, eliciting the self-indulgent illogic of the shooter George VI, quoted every week in the *Shooting Times,* that 'the wildlife of today is not ours to dispose of as we please. We have it in trust. We must account for it to those who come after'. Yet plainly not to the whole populace. Even Queen Victoria had frowned on her own son's shooting parties because they were socially exclusive, unlike fox hunting, where the rag- and bobtail at least got to follow the hounds on foot. Her views did not prevail. The then Prince of Wales spent £300,000 on turning Sandringham into a leading shoot, raising the annual bag from 7000 to 30,000, with a record day's partridge kill of 1342 on 10 November, 1905.

A Land Enquiry Committee Report lamented in 1913 that agricultural output was being held down because perhaps half of all farmland was devoted to game conservation. Although the Agricultural Holdings Act of 1908 had enabled tenants to claim compensation for damage, they protested they were likely to find their leases ended if they did so. Game in all its forms was the sorest point in what it is no hyperbole to call a fractured society. To sum up, we see a tradition hypothetically descending from the old squires but more realistically mirroring their ways, and becoming ever more tightly bound by the landowner control which the Restoration settlement made sure would never be challenged again. Blood sports have always persisted or recovered despite shifts in the most sought-after prey and despite all the shocks to which social change has subjected them.

'The past has not passed', says Adam Nicolson, 'Gentry consciousness knows no history'. It is a synthetic consciousness when new men buy tradition with hard cash, membership of sporting communities seldom being directly inherited. In Wiltshire, only three of the thirty-two houses that belonged to great landed families in 1877 remain in the hands of their descendants, though two others do own land nearby. Among the next class down, the gentry, only one family is still in possession and only then because a fortunate marriage to money from trade enabled the owner to buy back his estate, which had fallen into the hands of a chocolate manufacturer. As for the country at large, Nicolson gives an unexpectedly bright picture of continuity on the estates of the great lords but does not disguise the virtual collapse of landholding by the gentry, whose Tory sporting culture he describes in eloquent detail. No matter, new money continues to refresh blood sports, as it has for centuries.

Sources and Further Reading

Anon. (c.1938). *British sports and sportsmen: Shooting and deerstalking.* London: Sports & Sportsmen Ltd.

Bloch, M. (2009). *James Lees-Milne: The life.* London: John Murray.

Brander, M. (Ed.). (1972). *The international encyclopedia of shooting.* London: Rainbird Reference.

Cannadine, D. (2005). *The decline and fall of the British aristocracy.* London: Penguin.

Clarke, B. (2008). *On fishing.* London: Collins.

Cobbett, W. (1912). *Rural rides.* London: J. M. Dent & Sons.

Collins, T., et al. (Eds.). (2005). *Encyclopedia of traditional British rural sports.* London: Routledge.

Dahles, H. (1990). *Mannen in Het Groen: De wereld van de jacht in Nederland.* Nymegen: SUN.

Davis, E. L. (1978). *The story of an ancient fishery.* Hungerford: Trustees of the Town and Manor.

Gray, R. (2015, November 11). Lord Ripon's legendary shoot. *Shooting Times.*

Hayter, T. (2002). *Halford and the dry-fly revolution.* London: Robert Hale.

Jennings, L. (2010). *Blood knots: Of father, friendship and fishing.* London: Atlantic Books.

Longrigg, R. (1977). *The English squire and his sport.* London: Michael Joseph.

Mandler, P. (1997). *The fall and rise of the stately home.* New Haven: Yale University Press.

Moody, R. (2005). *Mr Benett of Wiltshire: The life of a county member of parliament 1773–1852.* East Knoyle: Hobnob Press.

Nickerson, J. (1989). *A shooting man's creed.* London: Sidgwick & Jackson.

Nicolson, A. (2011). *The gentry: Stories of the English.* London: HarperPress.

Robinson, P. *Pheasant shooting in Britain: The sport and the industry in the 21st century.* www.animalaid.org.uk

Ruffer, J. G. (n.d.). *The big shots: Edwardian shooting parties.* No place stated: Debretts Peerage.

CHAPTER 7

Living by Rapine & Plunder

Abstract The Game Laws protecting landowners' sporting quarry from poachers were strictly enforced by armies of gamekeepers. Two poaching incidents involving the same family on the Earl of Ailesbury's Wiltshire estate are described on the basis of unusual evidence, one in the 1780s and the other in the 1810s. In the first case, the Earl's corrupt agent used circumstantial reports to secure a conviction against a small farmer but this was overturned when another man confessed. The laws were savage but judges still paid attention to legal form when giving judgement. In the second case, a gang of unemployed young men (the same farmer's sons) were transported to Australia, less because of the verdict against them than because members of the local elite wished to rid the district of them.

Keywords Earl of Ailesbury • Gamekeepers • Poaching • Transportation to Australia • Wiltshire

In January 1780, the Earl of Ailesbury received a letter from one of his agents concerning the gamekeepers in Savernake Forest, Wiltshire: 'they have certainly been pretty much harrassed (sic) of late in watching at nights frequently after a hard day's work; but necessary it is, since the Villains have taken to Shooting Pheasants by night.' Poachers faced visible temptations,

E. L. Jones, *Landed Estates and Rural Inequality in English History*,
Palgrave Studies in Economic History,
https://doi.org/10.1007/978-3-319-74869-6_7

for the agent added that 'I was sorry to see, as I came through Hor wood common 9 o'clock thursday night, pheasants perched on boughs, that I could scarcely frighten off, tho' a full moon and snow on the ground made it almost as light as day—one might shoot one with a pistol'.

For centuries the practice of blood sports was matched by poaching carried on by sometimes violent men who refused to accept that they should be excluded from woods, fields and wild life, and whose families needed all the protein they could get. The elite responded by hiring armies of gamekeepers. Game Laws protected landed property ever more stringently, imposing punishments for poaching up to hanging or transportation to the convict settlement at Botany Bay. The clash between the two sides has often been outlined and is sometimes illustrated by reports of particular episodes. Such accounts are inevitably third-party history, like looking back at unknown participants through a telescope. This chapter will provide a closer view of reality by turning to the microscope and revealing the personalities and contingencies hidden behind summarised historical writing: it will describe two linked poaching affairs on the Earl of Ailesbury's land. The coincidence of legal rules and severe retribution which is found is a paradox of particular note, seldom obvious in general accounts of crime and punishment.

During the 1780s security did not much improve on the Earl's Wiltshire estates. In January 1787, there were two outstanding poaching events. The *Salisbury Journal* described how a set of daring poachers, surprised in Horsell Coppice near Great Bedwyn by some of his Lordship's keepers, had 'cruelly beaten and almost murdered two of them'. But a poacher had been overpowered and another taken soon afterwards, while 'diligent search is making after the rest of the gang'. One keeper was in a 'dangerous way', vomiting continually, the other was cut about the head and bruised, and the pair had to be carried home in a cart. A poacher's gun had been seized, together with the broken butts of two more. An account of this fight is among the thousands of letters concerning the Earl's estates which are held in the Wiltshire and Swindon Record Office. It was written by the other agent, John Ward, who, eager to be scrupulous about ownership, signed off, 'I send your Lordship 3 Hen Pheasants wch the Poachers had killed.'

The Horsell poachers had clearly not been put off by another affray earlier the same month or by the enquiries, searches and offers of rewards for information that were roiling the countryside in its wake. Although the other incident did not match the struggle at Horsell for brutality, its circumstances constituted in Ward's eyes a greater affront than the bashing of a couple of gamekeepers. On 9 January he described it as a 'most atrocious offence'. It took place in Southgrove, a large, isolated wood not far outside Savernake Forest and also part of Lord Ailesbury's estate. The Southgrove case is the first of the two we shall study. Some of its progress is recorded in patches of close detail, other parts are left obscure. Further obscurity arises because, of the people involved, four pairs had remarkably similar names. This extraordinary set of duplications is ignored here for fear of bringing confusion to what is already a complicated tale.

Much of the two stories that follow concerns a family called Tarrant. Although one incident took place in 1787 and the other in 1818, they are linked because this family was involved in both, the very link exposing how the landed system and its antagonists operated. On the Saturday before the Horsell affair—in itself peripheral to this story—a gang of poachers had arrived at Southgrove, declaring they meant to have a night's diversion among the pheasants. Leaving two of their number to hold the keeper, his wife and son indoors, the others shot all night. The two men left on guard kept the Southgrove gamekeeper in his house, threatening to blow his brains out, and swearing 'in a most horrid maner (sic)'. As soon as this was reported to him, the agent, Ward, printed a notice offering £50 for information and by that means was able to obtain a witness and close the matter to his own satisfaction. By March he was certifying to Lord Ailesbury that men from both the Horsell and Southgrove gangs had been tried and declared guilty. The man accused of being the ringleader at Southgrove was called John Tarrant and although other witnesses had been brought to alibi him. Ward assured his employer, 'the prisoners knew they were swearing falsely'. A lawyer involved in the case, Edward Montague, likewise wrote to Lord Ailesbury, 'I should pay no regard to any Affidavits such a Gang of Villains should offer to make. They would not from me obtain the least degree of Credit... It is laughable to hear such a Set of Rascals, confessing their own guilt, in living by Rapine & Plunder, talking about their fine Feelings & Depression of Spirits'.

Of the two men charged over Southgrove, John Tarrant was considered the more culpable because he had recruited others and because he owned some property. Transgressions by anyone with a recognisable place in rural society were always infuriating to those in authority. Tarrant protested his innocence and declined to find sureties for his appearance at the assizes, which was probably why he was gaoled at Salisbury to await trial. When the case came up, Mr. Justice Buller, a notoriously harsh judge, gave it as his opinion that Tarrant had advertised his guilt by running away, changing his coat and locking himself in. Moreover, the court was told that the Earl had already paid it a compliment by presenting the gang member who testified against Tarrant with the £50 reward in advance, so that he could not be suspected of being biased through hope of further gain.

According to John Ward, the judge had heard the prosecution's *strong* evidence with approval—the 'strong' was emphasised. Ward himself had accompanied the Southgrove gamekeeper's wife to the gaol, where they saw John Tarrant standing among thirty or forty prisoners. She picked him out as the man who had forced his way into her house with a gun and her son testified that the voice he had heard was Tarrant's. Beyond that, the judge was persuaded by the informer, who was able to voice the threats Tarrant had supposedly made.

Tarrant's own witnesses seemed to contradict one another but the Counsel recommended not trying them for perjury: punishments for poaching needed to be harsh enough to form a deterrent but the Counsel thought it undesirable that the public should be further inflamed against the Game Laws. Ward himself was relieved that the punishments meted out had not stirred up the usual 'prejudice' against the laws, possibly because people were disposed to regard anything involving gun crime as a serious breach of law and order. He expressed his 'Infinite Satisfaction' that Tarrant was sentenced to three years in gaol and would be released only if he paid an additional fine of £20 and gave sureties for good behaviour for a further seven years. Ward even had something up his sleeve should Tarrant escape conviction—another warrant to oblige him to pay £5 and keep him confined for an additional three months.

The earliest sign that all was not well with the prosecution was a murmuring throughout the district that Tarrant and his companion were innocent. Poachers from Ludgershall, Wiltshire, were heard boasting that they had been the ones responsible for Southgrove. Ward acknowledged this in a letter to the Earl, while insisting on the validity of the evidence he had gathered. The affair seemed sewn up. In the *Salisbury Journal* for 2 July, 1787, there was however a report that turned the matter on its head: 'His Majesty has been pleased at the instance of the Earl of Ailesbury, to grant his most gracious pardon to Tarrant... adjudged a long imprisonment, for a most daring assault on his Lordship's woodmen, at South Grove.' The formalities incorporated in a system of savage punishments were shown by the addition of a face-saving note. This was to the effect that 'His Lordship was induced to intercede in their behalf, from a suggestion that some recent discoveries have rendered the evidence... rather doubtful, though perfectly satisfactory, at the time, to the grand and petty juries, as well as to the learned judge'.

What had tripped up John Ward was a remarkable intervention, combined with the formality of legal procedure. Justice there may not have been but rules there were. We are accustomed to thinking of the legal system during the eighteenth century as harsh and bigoted, especially when concerning the Game Laws. Harsh it was: magistrates who were themselves landowners adjudicated on offences affecting their own estates and gamekeepers had been known to haul captive poachers before a squire in his own parlour. If cases reached the judiciary they came before men who were sanctimonious, fond of their own voices, relentless in defence of property and downright cruel, as may be grasped from W. H. Hudson's classic *A Shepherd's Life*, where he condemns them as human devils. 'Their pleasure in passing dreadful sentences was very thinly disguised, indeed', Hudson wrote, 'by certain lofty conventional phrases as to the necessity of upholding the law, morality, and religion'. All this was true and it is cold comfort to learn that, although offences carrying the death penalty were multiplying in the early nineteenth century, the number of executions actually carried out was falling.

A type of mitigation nevertheless arose from the very legalism on which lawyers fed and the fine points they were happy to debate in court. Judges were fascinated by the niceties of the law, certainly more so than tipsy squires in their parlours. It was not entirely a charade. We should distinguish between the severity of the punishment once someone was convicted and the courtroom procedure whereby conviction was secured in the first place. The legal system was not wholly without scruples, disproportionately vicious though its results could be. It was as rule-bound as playing chess with a giant in his castle—fair enough, as long as you did not lose.

On this occasion John Tarrant did not lose, though the costs he bore must have been heavy and helped to drive him from farming into labouring, souring him and cramping the prospects for his children. On this occasion his chestnuts were pulled out of the fire by an astonishing stroke of fortune. He had been languishing in gaol in Salisbury when a man called Lawrence turned up out of the blue. Edward Lawrence was a smuggler and claimed to have been overseas. On his return he hastened to give an account of having been at Southgrove—whether Tarrant had really been with him at the keeper's house we shall never know—and volunteered that he was the one who issued the threats. He did not want an innocent man to take the rap.

Lawrence testified before a Berkshire MP and other gentlemen to the effect that he had recruited a 'high spirited bunch' of youths from Ludgershall. They bought powder and shot in Hungerford, liquor at the Chequers Inn and proceeded to Southgrove, where, according to Lawrence, the gamekeeper was actually injured. At least this explained reports stressed by John Ward that a gang had been heard moving between Hungerford (and the next village of Froxfield, where Tarrant lived) and South Grove. The irony was that the gang failed to kill as many pheasants as they hoped, 'the night being too dark for their purposes'. Two further witnesses to Tarrant's innocence were now accepted and grounds for clemency proposed. They were: serious doubts about the identification of Tarrant by the keeper's wife, who was held to be 'a Woman of weak Capacity', and that a Froxfield miller had overheard John Ward persuading her to say that she recognised Tarrant. A second witness had been bribed by Ward, who was described as 'a worthless Scoundrel', and the miller himself had been tempted with a bribe of £5. The conviction was blown out of the water. A report containing the details was prepared by Mr. Justice Buller, who felt he had been taken for a ride and in his own court at that.

John Ward was the leading banker in Marlborough as well as the Earl of Ailesbury's agent. His behaviour shows how readily a rule-bound and blandly moralising system could be corrupted but his defeat in this case also shows the underlying scepticism about authority in rural society. Besides straining to have 'Tarrant & his Gang' convicted, Ward was the ultimate sycophant and a not unsuccessful one. He was related to influential nonconformists but made sure his son received from the Earl preferment as Anglican vicar of Great Bedwyn and that a relative was made perpetual curate of another village.

The case of another poacher at this period is further evidence of Ward's lack of scruples and hankering for dominion over the neighbourhood. This poacher had two convictions, was in debt and had had the temerity to escape from prison. Recaptured, he was awaiting conviction, during which time, lamented Ward, my Lord must supply him with bread, 'for his Friends about the Forrest will furnish his table with Game, & his smugling (sic) Acquaintance, with Gin'. In any age, the socially ambiguous role of land agents lent itself to scornful attitudes like these and sometimes to the holding of more extreme views than their employers. It is a variant of the 'agency problem' in which the interests of an underling do not so much diverge from as exaggerate the interests of his boss. Ward was an example of this and in the event did not suffer much for his mistakes, despite having been tagged as a 'worthless Scoundrel' and despite one letter in the archives that describes his personal affairs as precarious. His successor as agent really did go too far and carried out repairs on the estate only along routes the Earl might be expected to travel, a bit like erecting a Potemkin village, but that man was found out and sacked.

After John Tarrant had been almost miraculously pardoned, he opened war on the preservers of game, co-opting his sons when they grew up. The battleground extended for miles around his home at Oakhill, a hamlet in Froxfield, and spilled over from Wiltshire into next-door Berkshire. Obviously we can discover only the cases when he and members of his family were caught, and probably not all of these.

Thirty years after Southgrove, the Tarrants finally overreached themselves, and when what amounted to a little collective biography of five of John Tarrant's sons and one of his nephews was compiled, it was penned on a convict ship when they were transported to New South Wales. For members of what had become a labouring family to supply any biographical sketch is most unusual. It notes that John Tarrant had been involved in poaching pheasants. His offspring poached all the time, pheasants, hares, trout, no matter. They were caught more and more often, but it took the corruptible—and in their case corrupted—legal system a long time to rid the countryside of them.

Most of their offences were for poaching pheasants and an occasional hare. The year 1817 saw offences rise to a national crescendo because demobilised servicemen had come back to villages where there was not enough work during the depression after the Napoleonic Wars. In that year, various Tarrants and Thomas Pithouse (a cousin) were fined or gaoled for poaching. In March, Fulwar Craven, a relative of Lord Craven at Ashdown Park, convicted Thomas Tarrant of 'using a certain Engine called a Wire in the Parish of Shalborne, Berks for the Destruction of Game'. (Wires were snares and even simple devices like that were called 'engines'). The Tarrants added stealing fish to their crimes in 1817, usually going to poach on the river Kennet. This was a river that had been praised by topographers for its trout and crayfish since the sixteenth century and it is no surprise that the banks were closely watched. In May Young John Tarrant, that is to say John Tarrant junior of Froxfield, got six months for poaching fish from the Kennet yet returned to crime the minute he was released from gaol. The Tarrants might reasonably have been called disorderly. They would not go willing. In almost every instance the charges brought against them were for crimes against the Game Laws, although sometimes for assaults on men trying to arrest them.

Then, in October 1818, five Tarrant brothers and Thomas Pithouse committed an offence that finally had them sent to New South Wales as convicts. They were sentenced for stealing chicken in the Berkshire parish of Ashbury. The Quarter Sessions' charge was that the gang had lifted 'six cocks of the price and value of sixpence and six hens of the price and value of fourpence', but there was a pheasant involved too and it was this that brought them under the purview of the Game Laws. Less than ten days after one of Old John's sons, Lewis, had been discharged from gaol he had gone to Faringdon hiring fair in Berkshire with three of his brothers, a cousin and another man. On their way home they committed the offence for which they were transported—stealing chicken and a hen pheasant at Ashbury, a village on Lord Craven's estate, dropping the birds and some snares as they ran.

The head gamekeeper had previously found snares set along a droveway at Idstone, which was a hamlet in Ashbury. Expecting that the poachers would come back for them, he paid some men to hide overnight in the ditch and hedgerow on either side of the drove. He had six men with him, one of whom, a gamekeeper, was Stephen Jones (my own three times great-grandfather). Before dawn the next morning seven men came across Idstone Field from the direction of Arkell's Hill Barn. When they drew opposite to the waiting party, three of those in hiding rushed out. The poachers ran off, but one of the gang called Gough soon puffed to a halt and was captured. Once Gough had been secured, and doubtless acting on his information, the head keeper fetched his horse and tracked the Tarrants over the downs to Froxfield, asking along the way if anyone had seen them. Exactly how and when they were taken into custody is nowhere reported but Young John Tarrant, who had not been with his brothers at Idstone, went to gaol for three months for resisting their arrest. We should add that two years later, nothing daunted or maybe just desperate, two other Pithouses, labourers of Froxfield, were prosecuted for stealing fish.

The depositions in the case are mostly concerned with the details of the theft and its prelude when the Tarrants had been carousing in the Cross Keys pub. Most of the culprits were in the Bridewell when they were formally identified. Six of them, Pithouse and the Tarrants, including a brother who had not been present at Ashbury, were transported. Gough vanishes from history. No doubt he took his reward and changed his name; the Game Laws produced numbers of turncoats like him, so great was the reward and so dire the alternative. Gough may even have calculated his chances in advance and joined the gang in order to spy on it. William Cobbett said the countryside was full of such spies.

The most outrageous document among the depositions was a petition, or draft petition, from local magistrates to the Home Secretary, positively begging that the Tarrants be 'sent out of the country'. The request was doubtfully legal. The Game Laws may have demanded seven years' transportation as a penalty for being found with a pheasant and snares, but which individual was responsible? Niceties were no longer in the magistrates' minds. They wanted to cleanse the country of these people, although according to P. B. Munsche, an authority on the Game Laws in general and Wiltshire in particular, the aim was usually to make examples rather than to ship out every criminal. A cowed population was the goal.

The Froxfield culprits were transported to Australia on a convict ship called the 'John Barry', on which also happened to travel Commissioner Thomas Bigge and his secretary. Bigge had been sent out to New South Wales by Lord Bathurst on a commission of enquiry to discover why convicts were openly choosing to be sent to Botany Bay. Bathurst charged Bigge with making sure the colonies were to be dreaded, the type of thinking that created the hell of Port Arthur in Tasmania. Bigge whiled away some of the voyage by asking the prisoners why they had opted to be transported when they might have stayed in the hulks in an English harbour (which in practice meant digging gravel at Portsmouth for sixteen hours a day). Even given that wretched alternative, the journey to Australia was a stark risk and on the face of it difficult for prisoners to assess. Bigge recorded the clues the Tarrants supplied about their choice; these suggested they knew more about Australia than might have been expected of village lads.

A twist in the tale is implicit in the Tarrants' replies to Commissioner Bigge on shipboard. One of them called Decimus stated that he had 'heard a good account of it'. He had not even been present at the Ashbury incident but reportedly asked to go to New South Wales with his brothers. Young men reduced, as likely as not, to working on the roads in England for a parish pittance, were perhaps free from the worst fears of transportation. They had less to lose than might be thought. In addition, the Tarrant brothers included former soldiers and seamen who had travelled and presumably learned from the military grapevine about the reasonableness of Governor Macquarie's Sydney. This endorsement of the Botany Bay colony was not what Lord Bathurst had hoped to hear.

On the face of it, the Tarrant brothers were several times unlucky to be transported to New South Wales. Unlucky, first, in that the family at Oakhill had suffered agricultural troubles in the late eighteenth century: in her will of 1770 Grace Pocock of North Standen, Hungerford, left James Tarrant (John's father, the boys' grandfather) his estate—a little farm— which she said he had been obliged to sign over to her for a loan of £200. Unlucky, next, to be single men in the age group that found work so hard to come by after the Napoleonic Wars, when married men took precedence. Third, out of luck to fall foul of the increasingly severe Game Laws, to be caught, convicted, sentenced and then to find themselves among the fraction actually dispatched to Australia. They were taken from Reading gaol to the hulks at Portsmouth at two o'clock in the morning one Monday in January 1819, an hour coldly calculated to reduce the chances of anyone trying to rescue them. Yet the long-term outcome was actually a lucky one, for the family has flourished in Australia.

SOURCES AND FURTHER READING

Bathe, G. (2015). Rotten sticks and shameful outrages: Desperation and crime near Bedwyn. *Wiltshire Local History Forum, 17*, no pagination.

Hopkins, H. (1986). *The long affray: The poaching wars in Britain*. London: Macmillan.

Hudson, W. H. (1936). *A Shepherd's life*. London: J. M. Dent & Sons.

Jefferies, R. (1949). *Wildlife in a southern county*. London: Lutterworth Press.

Jefferies, R. (1978). *The gamekeeper at home; The amateur poacher*. Oxford: Oxford University Press.

Jefferies, R. (1987). *Round about a great estate*. Bradford-on-Avon: Ex Libris Press.

Jones, E. L. (2016). Poaching crimes near Great Bedwyn: A more complete account. *Wiltshire Local History Forum, 18*, no pagination.

Munsche, P. B. (1981). *Gentlemen and poachers: The English game laws 1671–1831*. London: Cambridge University Press.

Osborne, H., & Winstanley, M. (2006). Rural and urban poaching in Victorian England. *Rural History, 17*(2), 187–212.

The Marquess of Ailesbury. (1962). *A history of Savernake forest*. Privately printed.

CHAPTER 8

Institutions and Inequality in the Countryside

Abstract The broad hierarchical structure of rural society has been similar for centuries. In southern England the main counter-currents were the slow drift of industry to the northern coalfields and the interruptions brought about by the agricultural depression that lasted with little break from 1880 to 1940. Labour was deskilled by the former process and impoverished during the latter because it failed to migrate fast enough. Against these trends nothing significant was done, either by landowners or by the clergy. Estates and landed society have persisted up to the present by adopting a variety of devices. An associated debate concerns whether or not social institutions have been economically efficient or (as argued here) primarily concerned to redistribute wealth to the owners of land.

Keywords Efficiency of social institutions • Deskilling of labour • Redistribution of wealth • Social hierarchies

The rural economy was organised around market towns spaced perhaps fourteen miles apart right across the country. These towns were each accessible on foot from the surrounding area. They processed farm products and arranged for their shipment to larger markets, especially London. They serviced local agriculture with blacksmiths, wheelwrights, waggon builders and the like, and supplied the farm community with goods imported from the manufacturing sector. During the eighteenth century small town society expanded, became prosperous and secured Improvement Acts to develop roads, public facilities and amenities. The frequency of settlement fires, which had been recurrent and devastating, fell away steeply once tile or slate roofs replaced flammable thatch. Although we should not take the surviving buildings as representative, given that the worst back-alley cottages have been swept away, Georgian towns were attractive places, particularly when contrasted with their rustic predecessors. They shared with neighbouring estates the task of organising the affairs of rural England.

This 'urban renaissance' has been seen as instrumental in toning down the antagonisms lingering after the Civil Wars. Middle-class demand came to equal or surpass that of the upper classes. Gentry patronage did nevertheless remain significant, although in the late eighteenth century it started shifting to London and the spa towns, partly as a consequence of transport improvements. Quakers and nonconformists (especially Baptists) were economically active in the market towns, though it now paid them to concentrate on milling, malting, brewing, trading and banking whereas manufacturing slowly faded in the face of cheaper goods imported from larger towns or the North. London was growing and was served by a whole ring of towns that found it profitable to specialise in gathering, processing and shipping the products of the land.

When transport improved as a result of better roads, canals and railways, an increasing proportion of the best-paying functions began to concentrate in the larger towns. The market towns suffered from import competition as the larger towns and their factories gained from economies of scale and undercut the prices of goods made in small places. Local guilds had a zero-sum view of the world and responded to competition by continuing to restrict entry to particular occupations and sharing out what trade was left, though with diminishing success. The institutions of the market towns accordingly found it hard to adapt; they became backwaters with backwoods societies to match. This became very evident during the agricultural depression of the late nineteenth century. Towns dependent on their agricultural surrounds then marked time and their economies were progressively less capable of vigorous adjustment. What had been lively little places one or two centuries earlier became close to stagnant, with reduced incentives or opportunities for entrepreneurship and a gradual outflow of the brighter children.

There had been a creditable scatter of early scientific and technical innovations in the countryside but the shift in the centre of gravity of manufacturing to London, the Midlands and the North undermined the potential for adopting them in the increasingly rural South. The northwards relocation actually predated much industrial use of coal, domestic heating being the more important initial source of demand. Northern industries were already expanding through the energy of their populations, especially in towns with weak corporations and little regulation. They learned to employ cheap coal in a range of technologies that could not be matched in the South—after all the North had coal on the doorstep. Nor were the Southern landed classes enamoured of manufacturing on their doorsteps and they discouraged or even stifled it.

The fact that industry grew in the North encourages the conventional but anachronistic view that northern coal was what destroyed southern industry. Yet the presence or absence of coal—undeniably vast as its effects were to prove—was simply not the initial or sole determinant of the South's rural turn. Byron Rogers quotes a local man on why Northamptonshire did not turn industrial after iron ore was found there in 1852: 'it was the dukes. They owned everything and they loved the land and they loved foxhunting. They wanted nothing to change.' As Field Marshall Wavell said when horrified by the unethical behaviour in Britain during the late 1940s, 'unless we can get back to something like our old standards of honesty, family morality, hard work, and pride in craftsmanship, I do not feel we shall maintain our position or regain our former prosperity, which was founded on the above qualities: more, for instance, than on the fortuitous location of coal and iron-ore in the British Isles'. This was an astute observation about the ultimate basis of economic activity.

The decay of local manufacturing meant that labour in the South was slowly being deskilled during the eighteenth and nineteenth centuries. English society, especially rural society, had always involved top-down social control and a massive waste of talent. The celebrated stained glass windows put up by a nouveau riche merchant in the church at Fairford, Gloucestershire, about 1500 told the Bible story to those who could not read—as an alternative to providing them with proper schools. The use of Latin in court books had been abandoned under the Commonwealth but was resumed after 1660, once more excluding those without an education in classical languages. Thomas Jefferson wrote that William & Mary College should nurture 'those talents which nature has sown as liberally among the poor as the rich, but which perish without use, if not sought for and cultivated'. But that was in another country and, as the saying goes, the Americans waste things and the English waste people. Jefferson's opinion would have been thought heretical in England long after his day. Investment in education there was extremely limited, though the trend was not quite uniform. When there were signs of a labour shortage during the early eighteenth century the Charity School movement did make some temporary amends, but literacy fell again about 1800, when the population was growing fast. One of the more aggravating features of the society was the manner in which the employing class scoffed at efforts by its 'inferiors' to better themselves, as when the Victorian incumbent of Sparsholt, Hampshire, derided his parish clerk for 'various mis-pronunciations peculiar to the race'. It did not concern the Rev. Heathcote that this was a result of inadequate educational institutions nor that lack of skills would hold back the whole economy. Such men, in comfortable circumstances themselves, were more intent on maintaining a social hierarchy that was in their interests.

The role of the established church in all this was unfortunate: it was inextricably part of the reigning system, up to and including the absentee pluralists who collected parishes and farmed them out to curates, and the 'squarsons' who were concerned with hunting rather than parish work. The massive size of many rectories cannot be equated with good works nor can the vaunting tablets on the walls in memory of past incumbents be taken as signs of Christian humility. Published letters by clergy and their wives show their incomprehension of the plight of the poor and their complete acceptance of society as it was. They demonstrate the unbridgeable divide between pastor and flock. The clergy's frame of reference saw villagers as 'little people', almost a different species; the phrase was still current among the middle classes in the late twentieth century.

Before Victoria came to the throne the Evangelicals were starting to clean up society but at the cost of an unforgiving conformity. Churches were gloomy, macabre places, as they had been since the Reformation expunged colour from them. Sermons were often based on casuistic interpretations of the Bible and aimed to reinforce the existing social structure. H. E. Bates tells us it was the war of 1914–1918 which 'shattered church and squirearchy to bits'. They retained influence but lost power. Small wonder the squire slumbered in his private pew. Squire or incumbent, these men in their little kingdoms were free from ordinary social constraints and it is not particularly odd that they became odd themselves: tales of their eccentricity are legion. Hugh Barrett saw that plenty of the parsons in interwar Suffolk were frankly barmy.

Upper-class women of the nineteenth century sometimes expressed a dislike of maids who could read, lest they read their employers' letters. Harriet Martineau, supposedly a reformer, insisted that she intended educating people to be no more than servants. This was during the mood of fear about the doctrines of the French Revolution but persisted as a result of the self-interest of the employing classes. Samuel Wilberforce, Bishop of Oxford, proclaimed in 1857 that if everyone became learned and unsuited for the plough, 'the rest of us would have nothing to eat'. Cheap, docile and ignorant were the qualities desired in workers and servants. We noted earlier that the first names of people hired as domestics were likely to be changed to generic forms. In the larger houses, as one servant reported, they could be treated as replaceable items of furniture and just as easily moved or discarded.

Despite the lauding of William Wilberforce as an anti-slavery campaigner, an author of the day (stretching a moderately long bow perhaps) wrote that he wished the 'labouring poor were half as well off as the Negroes' and that 'we should in the first instance restore freedom to, and relieve the want of our own poor'. Whatever they achieved in suppressing slavery overseas, the social reformers neglected the suffering of the rural poor in their own country. Innumerable testimonies exist to the reality. The books of reminiscence that crowd the shelves of public libraries might be thought descriptive of the twilight era of rural England when agriculture was in depression, cottages and their thatch in disrepair (something evident in books of old photographs) and poverty prevalent. Despite social decay often passed off as picturesque, life was not quite as grim as it had been during the earlier era of mantraps and spring guns but nevertheless remained dismal enough. After the Repeal of the Corn Laws in 1846 living standards had been raised a little by a cheaper loaf and the health of a generation began to improve. This marginal advance was just discernible to an observer like Richard Jefferies.

An observation of the 1860s is the more persuasive because it was recounted by an American visitor, Elihu Burritt, who in *A Walk from London to Land's End* repeats the life story of a man he met trimming a hedge between Swindon and Marlborough. Married for thirty years, this man had never had a fresh piece of beef or mutton cooked under his roof. His daughter's family, with six children, lived on bread without cheese. Burritt thought that ultra-low wages were short-sighted on the part of the employing farmers, who would have to pay for it in poor rates when the men were old and infirm—short-sighted from the narrowest point of self-interest, 'to say nothing of moral principle and sentiment'. He calculated how much more farmers could afford to pay and what the benefit might be in terms of productivity. No remedy was in fact forthcoming either from reason or principle but only from the workings of the market, where in Burritt's day a slight labour shortage was just starting to raise wages a jot.

The estate system within which the labourers existed was at its height about 1870, by which date landowners had long been actively buying any land that came on the market. The New Domesday of 1873 showed that four-fifths of the British Isles were owned by just 7000 people out of a population of over 30 million, a distribution as unequal as anywhere in Europe with the *possible* exceptions of Romania and Austro-Hungary. The fortunes of the system had not however been without perturbations whenever it was hit by exogenous shocks. These, even 'the year without a summer' in 1816, do not loom large in national histories, which concentrate on human agency as if the natural environment were an inert backcloth. Admittedly, humanity's wars were equally great shocks and more prolonged too. The Napoleonic wars brought upsets that trailed on well after Wellington's victory at Waterloo in 1815.

Waterloo saw the defeat of an imperial despot but rather than reshape the world, as Napoleon had tried to do, the victors made Europe safe for reactionary aristocrats for another century. Wellington was presented with an estate at Stratfield Saye, Hampshire, where he was no more tender to local interests than any other great proprietor. The countryside, and to a large extent the country, continued to be run by a landed elite that had been shaken in the saddle but not unhorsed by events in Revolutionary and Napoleonic France. A tourist's guide of the mid-nineteenth century observed that Southern England had remained 'an uneventful economy' ever since Monmouth's failed rebellion of 1685—the Last Labourers' Revolt did not rate a mention. Accordingly, aristocrats dominated England after 1815 as they had before, when it had been possible for them to reach the pinnacle of prime minister. In the 1760s the Duke of Grafton, when prime minister, had openly cavorted with his mistress; plus ça change, he was a great-great-grandson of Charles II. Victoria's reign was perhaps more discreet rather than fundamentally different.

Great sections of the apparently ironclad social system did slowly begin to rust with the Repeal of the Corn Laws in 1846. As far as the agricultural economy was concerned, the most fundamental shock, when it came, was the late nineteenth century's flood of imported grain. Delayed for a generation, as much for lack of transport as anything, imports proved catastrophic to the arable districts, though clearly advantageous to the buyers of a cheaper loaf. Ruinously wet harvests at the end of the 1870s reinforced the blow. English grain growers could seldom compete with cheap cereals from overseas. Thistles grew in the fields, farms deteriorated or went untenanted, cottages were left unrepaired and farmworkers were without work. The system took heavy losses and staggered but did not fall. The historian John Kenyon tells us that rural destitution remained the preoccupation of Liberal governments after the 1890s. Villagers, he said, 'were still virtually helots' in 1911. R. H. Tawney wrote about the 'blind, selfish, indomitable aristocracy of county families' in tones quite different from the bloodless histories of a century later, written by academics who share neither his experience nor his moral fervour. Only between the two world wars did governments make an effort at rural slum clearance although in the event some of the properties listed were merely smartened up rather than demolished. The threadbare countryside was well depicted in the realist literature of the time and can be viewed in a freely available video about conditions in rural Oxfordshire during the Second World War, under the title *Twenty-four Square Miles*.

The potential dividend of labour moving from country to town was muted. Industry, now challenged by German and American manufacturing, could not absorb enough displaced workers and by Edwardian times much capital was instead exported to the colonies. The outflow of rural labour, though marked, was not enough to do much towards raising farm wages. In Southern England, rural labour remained downtrodden, with young children employed in the fields on tasks like clearing away stones. (This dreary work continued into the late 1950s.) Village teachers commonly lamented the withdrawal of children from school to go potato picking but for decades farmers' interests in cheap workers were served by making it possible to quit school a year early by passing the so-called Labour Exam. Hard-pressed parents were willing to oblige. The deplorable condition of education for the children of nineteenth-century farmworkers and the concern to limit what they could learn to simple matters likely to be useful to the farmers are detailed by Alastair Geddes in a booklet on Samuel Best and the Hampshire labourer. Samuel Best made sure that the school in his own parish taught the sons of farmers and of labourers side by side, but his liberal views on access to education were too advanced for the time and he was unable to persuade others in the clergy to adopt them.

Sixty years of agricultural depression from the late 1870s, interrupted by only a few years during and after the First World War, crippled many a landlord. Year after year, local newspapers offered standing timber for sale as the only realisable asset apart from the shooting. Tenants were hard to find and did not always possess enough capital when they were found. On the Worcestershire-Herefordshire border the majority of estates partly or wholly changed hands, an experience repeated in other districts. Almost eighty mansions were pulled down in England between 1870 and 1919 and those left standing were often in an even more parlous condition after the Second World War. The non-pecuniary rewards of proprietorship had not been enough to offset the financial drain. The actual membership of the landowning class altered and there was further turnover because some of the replacements could not sustain the outgoings. But it was a section of the personnel rather than the entire system that changed.

Recovery of a sort had begun quite early but was intermittent. The most visible and prolonged inflow was that of rich cotton and other manufacturers who had been moving south ever since the start of the nineteenth century. A number of Quaker industrialists upgraded themselves into landownership. Even the free-trader, John Bright, who was not socially acceptable (he was laughed at in the Commons for mispronouncing the Pytchley Hunt) had a Quaker brother-in-law who bought the Miserden estate in Gloucestershire. A surprising number of aristocrats repaired their finances by marrying American heiresses and other Americans bought estates outright.

As for arable farms, a brief prosperity did not outlast the withdrawal of First World War government support in 1922. Incomers from Scotland and the West Country began replacing the bankrupt farmers of South-central England, practising stricter economy and switching to dairying until demand for home-grown cereals in the Second World War restored the profitability of growing grain. Afterwards subsidies were provided under the 1947 Agriculture Act and continued under the Common Agricultural Policy of the European Union. This ensured there was no return to the environmentally attractive but socially deprived countryside of the interwar years. Without subsidies, however, arable farming would scarcely be sustainable today and international comparisons show productivity in UK farming to be lagging and inefficient.

Farm subsidies and income from leisure activities (opening the house to the public or selling places on shoots) bring in enough money nowadays to make the long depression and two wars seem almost transient in retrospect, just as the Cromwellian era proved only a passing interruption of common practice. The author of *Tom Brown's Schooldays* remarked that in his day the larger estates were held by people who had grabbed what was going, but Thomas Hughes had romantic ideas about the caste of small landowners from which he sprang. Admittedly the ownership of the soil is no longer as unequal as it was in his mid-Victorian times because so many tenants were able to buy their farms in later depressions when their landlords were financially embarrassed. New money still comes in to buy country houses and the status attached to them. What is more, 200 new country houses were erected in England between 1950 and 1980, a surprising figure given the lamentations about the demolishing of mansions in the fifteen years following the Second World War. But modern houses often have little associated farmland. Status derives more from the mansion than the land, though more monetary value attaches to house and land together. There is a 10 per cent premium over the price of the two valued separately which is the 'marriage value' from owning country house, landed estate and sporting rights combined.

The traditional sense of entitlement has been restored to anyone who owns rural property—even if they scarcely do more than drive a Land Rover or in view of the pointed findings of Dacher Keltner, a Mercedes! The *Financial Times* (31 December, 2015) cites a 2010 study for *Country Life* showing that over one-third of the land in the United Kingdom continues to be owned by the aristocracy and landed gentry. A new twist, or rather an old twist on a new, vast and chilly scale, has come about through the purchase of estates by foreign money. Richard Fortey's *The Wood for the Trees* (2016) remarks on this with respect to the Henley district. One estate there is now owned by a Russian and almost every other has been bought by a single Swiss banker. Fortey laments that such people do not mix locally. 'What is different now', he says, 'is the exclusiveness of the landowners: they really *do* exclude'. *Noblesse oblige* may have been mainly a fiction in the past but there is precious little, or none, nowadays.

Estates have recovered their attractiveness, especially as a number of the largest in the country have been registered offshore to dodge UK taxes. The full extent of this manoeuvre is obscure, though something has been uncovered by Freedom of Information requests and leaks of financial documents. The largest example is a grouse moor in north Yorkshire. Among the attractions of owning estates, shooting figures prominently as it has for centuries. When the purchasers are not bred to blood sports, many soon defer to local norms, as incomers have always done, and as a case study of Admiral Sir Peter Warren's purchase of a Hampshire estate as long ago as 1747 nicely demonstrates. He enlarged the estate but his investment was not immediately profitable and it took years for its value to rise. He was wary of parcels of land that could not readily be sold because lawsuits hung over them. Meanwhile, like new landowners at all periods up to the present day, Warren embraced the landlubbers' pastimes of shooting and fishing. The park landscapes created by people like Warren remain widely admired but the opportunity costs of their Arcadian scenery are not factored into account.

The recurrence of similar motives for individuals to hold blocks of land ensured the long-term continuity of the system as a whole. Its survival surely makes English history unusual. Yet a novel feature appears. Instead of the land supporting the house, the house—meaning the outside money—has come to support the land, or the part of it retained for leisure and display. Another novelty is that the ancient bond between the big house and the church has snapped. The doors in the park walls giving the family private access across the churchyard are still there, but are now unused, their hinges rusted shut. Incoming families, usually urban and sometimes foreign, are rarely active members of the Church of England and accept no obligation to it. Even so, the decline of the service economy of the landed estate is less marked than might be expected, because domestic labour is replaced by cheap immigrants from Spain and Portugal or supplemented by tradesmen in white vans. Estate maintenance and game-keeping are bolstered by the adoption of new technologies, such as chain saws, four-wheel drives and quad bikes.

Beneath the historical workings of the landed system lies a deeper problem about the effect of the institutional arrangements of which it was so large a part. How should the topic be pursued? How far should we use economic analysis, with its timeless logic based (at least until the emergence of behavioural economics) on a priori assumptions about maximising? Despite economists' pejorative dismissal of participant evidence as anecdotal storytelling, eschewing the approach altogether would be needlessly restrictive. The exaggerated reliance of economists on mathematics, that is the manipulation of abstract symbols rather than the interrogation of actual sources, can prove unrealistic, yet argument too easily slips and slides without the concepts and categories of economics. Even so, the economic historian may be surprised to find how often the wayward actions of individuals and many a political contingency seem more persuasive explanations of both continuity and change. Considering this, the issue of the efficiency of eighteenth-century institutions may be debated with someone who admires them, Douglas Allen, the Canadian author of *The Institutional Revolution*.

Allen brings an illuminating handful of economic concepts to bear on what appear to him the strange conventions of our aristocratic ancestors. North American scholars such as him, reared in more market-oriented societies, tend to find the conventions bizarre when what they really seem is unfamiliar. Anyone growing up in England, with the legacy this implies, may find them objectionable but will not necessarily find them astonishing. Allen is impressed that a limited group of people oversaw the transformation of a small country into a vast empire but says there are few pertinent aristocrats left today. Nevertheless their number may not be the appropriate consideration. The absolute number of influential individuals currently at the top of the landed pyramid is secondary to the weight of their position. Great wealth, some of it from farm subsidies, as well as great influence, still attaches, say, to proprietors like the Duke of Westminster and if royalty be included Queen Elizabeth II and Prince Charles. A mere 36,000 people own over half of all rural land and ten among them own one million acres.

Following ideas derived from the theorist, Ronald Coase, Allen finds rationality informing practices that otherwise seem weird. For instance he proposes a rational basis for duelling. This form of Russian roulette created 'hostage capital' for new entrants, their willingness to risk their all in order to acquire top status signalling their trustworthiness and fitness for the upper reaches of society. Allen argues that, before the introduction of quantitative techniques associated with industrialisation, behaviour could not be adequately measured, so that roundabout devices, including duels, were devised to demonstrate that a man was acceptable because he was prepared to hazard his all. Before the end of the eighteenth century, Allen claims, such indirect proxies for measurement were indispensable. This seems to exaggerate previous arithmetical incapacity and disparage the ability of the powerful to gauge the reliability of underlings or new neighbours. The upper ranks of English society were quite small and it was surely possible to learn enough about newcomers from more visible signs. What the landed class mostly wanted to know—to judge from the ready reception of the cotton masters—was whether the newcomers were rich enough for the sons to make husbands for their own daughters. If the sons had been to leading public schools it was probably signal enough.

Hostage capital included country mansions despite the fact that life in them was boring, says Allen. It is true that some landowners' wives were bored by the countryside and were loud in their demands to spend time in the spa towns or take part in the London season. Men, on the other hand, had more options. For thrills they could hunt foxes or gamble; if they wanted pleasure they could drink with their companions or molest the maidservants; if they wanted cerebral pursuits they could in a few scholarly instances write books. Allen implies that big houses were eventually pulled down because they were inconvenient, which is not a fair picture of their fate when families were faced with heirs dead in the wars, vanishing rent rolls, damage by troops billeted in them and the impact of death duties. Nor does it gibe with the number of surviving mansions and the renewed vogue for building big country houses that followed right on the heels of the demolition era.

Economic rationality implies that institutions were purposefully constructed and the fact that they lasted a long time is taken to mean they served useful functions. This need not be so. Institutions may persist despite being socially suboptimal. Mutually sustained networks of social sanctions may preserve an institution that is harmful, at least to some groups. It may be rational for each individual to conform to the conventions for fear of censure. In the case of landed institutions, collateral damage befell many owners, indeed whole swathes of them during agricultural depressions. The system was a demonstration of the findings by Keltner which show that rich people too often, even characteristically, display endemic greed, cheating, dominance behaviour and lack of empathy. Behavioural economics would treat this constellation as an economic trait but it can equally be seen as a failure of ethics that sat ill with the profession of Christian beliefs.

On the hypothesis that eighteenth-century institutions were optimal, they might be said to have paved the way for economic growth. But this gives too much credence to the set of institutions that happened to exist during the early stages of growth and runs the risk of *post hoc ergo propter hoc*. One may admire the ingenuity of an argument that the institutions were purposeful but remain unpersuaded by the notion that aristocratic and gentry society had much real purpose or effect beyond rent seeking and redistributing society's resources into its own hands. The wastefulness surely blunted any positive effects. 'Farmer' George III may have had his imitators among the landed class, but there is scant evidence that a hobbyist taste for husbandry went far towards maximising national output. On the contrary there is abundant evidence that resources were dissipated in elite leisure pursuits and amenities. In any case, maximum output is not necessarily the same as optimal output.

SOURCES AND FURTHER READING

Allen, D. W. (2009). A theory of the pre-modern British aristocracy. *Explorations in Economic History, 46*, 299–313.

Allen, D. W. (2011). *The institutional revolution.* Chicago: University of Chicago Press.

Basu, K., Jones, E., & Schlicht, E. (1987). The growth and decay of custom: The role of the new institutional economics in economic history. *Explorations in Economic History, 24*, 1–21.

Bates, H. E. (1985). *In the heart of the country.* London: Robinson.

Dodd, W. E. (1935). The emerge (sic) of the first social order in the United States. *American Historical Review, 40*(2), 217–231.

Fergusson, B. (1961). *Wavell: Portrait of a soldier.* London: Collins.

Garne, R. O. (1984). *Cotswold Yeomen and sheep.* London: Regency Press.

Gwyn, J. (1974). *The enterprising admiral: The personal fortune of Admiral Sir Peter Warren.* Montreal: McGill-Queen's University Press.

Harris, M. (1969). *A kind of magic.* London: Chatto & Windus.

Hill, C. (1972). *God's Englishman: Oliver Cromwell and the English revolution.* London: Penguin.

Jones, E. L. (2017). *Small earthquake in Wiltshire: Seventeenth-century conflicts and their resolution.* Sutton Veny: Hobnob Press.

Kenyon, J. (1993). *The history men.* London: Weidenfeld & Nicolson.

Phelan, N. (1983). *The swift foot of time: An Australian in England 1938–1945.* Melbourne: Quartet Books.

Plumb, J. H. (1977). *The growth of political stability in England 1675–1725.* London: Palgrave Macmillan.

Southall, M. (1822). *A description of Malvern.* Malvern: Privately printed.

Swinford, G. (1987). *The jubilee boy.* Filkins: The Filkins Press.

Trigg, D. A. (1998). *Salt of the earth: The life and work of bygone farm labourers.* London: Minerva Press.

Verey, D. (Ed.). (1980). *The diary of a Cotswold Parson: Reverend F. E. Witts 1783–1854.* Gloucester: Alan Sutton.

Wade, J. (1820). *The black book or corruption unmasked!* London: Effingham Wilson.

Wagner, A. (1975). *Pedigree and progress: Essays in the genealogical interpretation of history.* London: Phillimore.

Williamson, J. G. (1987). Did English factor markets fail during the industrial revolution. *Oxford Economic Papers, 39*, 641–678.

Williamson, J. G. (1994). Leaving the farm to go to the city: Did they leave quickly enough? In J. A. James & M. Thomas (Eds.), *Capitalism in context* (159–182). Chicago: University of Chicago Press.

CHAPTER 9

The Estate System as Market Failure

Abstract The continuity of the estate system dates from the Restoration, even from the Interregnum, when earlier arrangements were confirmed. The relevant circumstances are rehearsed. Social stability was created and enforced: a better term might be social stagnation. Numerous instances are supplied of the poverty at the base of the system and the steep social hierarchy and economic stasis that rested on it. The negative implications of the continued sole ownership of very large blocks of land are discussed with respect to their derivation from the system's prolonged history and their remarkable adaptability. Although typically discussed in terms of shorter periods, the landownership saga is conceived here as a single narrative.

Keywords Contemporary estates • Economic stasis • Historical continuity • Rural poverty • Maintenance of social stability

After the Restoration the temper of rural society was Royalist and Puritan squires accommodated to it. A letter of 1688 from one of the daughters of the former Royalist rebel, John Penruddock, to her husband, Thomas Chafin, printed in the *Gentleman's Magazine* for 1817, describes the network of families who returned to prominence. She mentions the enormous stakes hazarded in gambling at a Blandford inn, showing that

Cavalier insouciance lived on. Royalist attitudes to church and tithes remained firm; Norfolk gentry were said to have rushed to support the Restoration settlement because they had heard of Quaker women challenging the levying of tithes.

No sign emerged of any serious intention by the rich and powerful to abolish inequality. Hope of that had died in 1649 with the Levellers shot in Burford. They probably knew there was little sympathy for them among those who mattered. Two years earlier, confronted by demands for one man, one vote, General Ireton had grumbled that, 'all the main thing that I speak for is because I have an eye to property'. Cromwell concurred: 'to give votes to men that have no interest but the interest of breathing, would be anarchy'. The Marxist, Christopher Hill, says that Cromwell 'presided over the great decisions which determined the future course of English and world history'. That included destroying any threat from forward-looking radicals like the Levellers as well as from backward-looking Royalists, in order to ensure the supremacy of Cromwell's own cohorts.

Whether Hill seriously thought that world history could be predicted from Cromwell's machinations in the 1650s is unclear. The American liberal historian, William E. Dodd, proposed a similar thesis, although he claimed it was the clique around Charles II in the 1660s which 'shifted the course of modern history'. Cromwell's supporter, Martin Noel, became a member of that powerful clique, which demonstrates continuity across the Restoration. To show that the 1650s or 1660s, or both together, determined centuries of future history plainly requires further argument. It needs a theory of path-dependence that neither Hill nor Dodd supplies or shows any sign of realising is required. Seen as logical necessities their propositions, standing alone, are too deterministic and quite unlikely. They are improbably fixed: later events of many types might have blown history in other directions. But what they say is descriptively plausible. Despite the conceptual emptiness of their claims, the Cromwellian and Restoration periods did jointly load the dice; later experience conformed to arrangements established at that time. This did not merely affect England but was long echoed in the social geographies of colonies to which the sons of English landowners migrated.

Little work on the social history of estates and landownership is critical in intent. Much is high-level gossip and it is necessary to read between the lines to bring into focus the misallocation of resources on which the system rested. The blind snobbery of the system may be seen in the mid-nineteenth-century work of Jane Loudon, described as the Mrs

Beeton of gardening: 'a lady, *with the assistance of a common labourer* to level and prepare the ground, may turn a barren waste into a flower-garden *with her own hands.*' (Italics added).

The purpose of this concluding chapter is to offer a panorama of landed society through the centuries. Mutations in society mean that whereas the dress of Victorian landowners, say, was different from that of Stuart times, similarities in their behaviour are always recognisable. Quite apart from subsequent continuities, the truth is that even the antagonistic regimes of the Civil War and Commonwealth periods had been far more alike than might be expected from the political and religious divisions. They relied on—and rewarded —some of the very same individuals. A perpetual feature under all regimes and rulers was the attraction of joining landed society via purchasing estates: investing non-agricultural money in land expanded and perpetuated the estate system. Some of its growth also arose from the habit of kings of co-opting support by creating additional peers, who usually were or became great landed proprietors. Occasional aristocratic lines might die out but their succession often continued, if need be through cousinly lines.

Parliament, stuffed with landowners, was also willing to reward the politically successful with grants, pensions and sinecures that were seldom if ever repealed, so that the system grew until in the view of nineteenth-century reformers it came to be a burden on the productive economy. As John Wade wrote in *The Black book,* 'the portion of every man's produce levied for the support of government, of pensioners, placemen, sinecurists, and standing armies, has invaded the funds necessary for the comfortable subsistence of the labourer, and for carrying on the trade, commerce, and agriculture of the kingdom'. From the second half of the seventeenth century government was or returned to being a massive rent-seeking machine.

Puritan bigwigs, up to and including Cromwell's own family, had feathered their nests while they had the chance. Lenthall, Speaker of the Commons, took bribes including a large estate at nowhere other than Burford where the Levellers were shot! The more corrupt the acquisition of Royalist estates by rich merchants and lawyers, which happened in a rush after the execution of Charles I in 1649, the greater the newcomers' urge to appear as established landed folk and marry into the aristocracy. They were the people who welcomed back Charles II, sometimes effusively—General Fairfax offered the king the chestnut mare he had ridden at the battle of Naseby and this remarkable but surely double-edged gift was accepted. Charles II's reign steadied the wheel of state of which these men had become spokes.

Establishment and parvenus fused but the fact that the temper of Restoration times was Royalist did not mean a return of all forfeited estates. Resuming one's lands, if they were recovered at all, could be an expensive business. The experience of Lord Arundell, a recusant or Roman Catholic, from Wardour, Wiltshire, is telling. He had been punished for acting as a second in a duel in which his brother-in-law was killed but obtained permission from Cromwell to take refuge in France. Many of his estates were thereupon sold to his uncle, Humphrey Weld, who had sufficiently purged his own recusancy to be permitted to buy his nephew's land. At the Restoration, Arundell did recover his property but it cost him £35,000 to do so. He was not the only one out of pocket. The witticism of the day was that at the Restoration Charles II passed an Act of Indemnity for his enemies but an Act of Oblivion for his friends.

The Restoration was an 'Elite Settlement' of a type rare but not unknown in world history—for instance, the end of conflict and installation of the Tokugawa shogunate in 1603 is well known to students of Japan. The shogun took the premier position, but the lords, daimyo, were left to run their domains subject to regular attendance at his court. Elite settlements were classically of this type, the sharing of power between a ruler and his subordinates. Although in the England of 1660 Charles II similarly came to terms with the Puritan elite and armed conflict was forsworn in favour of Puritans and Royalists living together and sharing the spoils, there was a difference. A further settlement was required between the factions who had been fighting one another. The question that had been fought over proved to have been only, 'whose slaves the people shall be'. The two sides blended again in the landed class from which both had sprung. This settlement confirmed the traditional structure of society and hence the distribution of wealth and income; the Glorious Revolution of 1688 accepted the arrangements.

As far as the countryside and rural social system were concerned, 1688 was not a decisive break after which, and only after which, property became secure. Landed property was held by means that were not so much secure as securely contestable, by which enigmatic phrase is implied that titles were rarely set in stone. A land market active enough to respond to movements in product prices was the need. Total security, absolute ownership, without the goal of profit, might have created a wholly fossilised countryside. This was avoided, partly because landowners or their agents were far from completely insensitive to profit. In any case, ownership could always be challenged in the courts, although those rich enough to fee lawyers for affirming their rights within the maze of archaic stipulations might reasonably expect to hold onto their estates. All attempts at a land registry that might have regularised property rights foundered, century after century. The land market operated within a remarkably confused context and the surprise is that it worked as well as it did. The unending conflicts about tithes are sufficient to demonstrate the perpetual saga of legal dispute or alternatively one can read Dickens, *Bleak House*, which was based on real cases in the unbelievably dilatory Court of Chancery. A reasonable conclusion is that the economic growth which occurred in the eighteenth and nineteenth centuries did so despite, as much as because of, the nature of property rights.

If further discussion of the landed system be stretched over the centuries since Cromwellian times, this should not be taken to imply that the trends were linear, with no reverses and without nuances, nor without an earlier history. The account would be overloaded by trying to capture every eddy of the advancing tide. Even so, the estate system as a whole stayed remarkably proof against the economic fluctuations and political interventions to which later times subjected them. This quasi-stability justifies a degree of looseness with chronology since similar behaviour recurred in different centuries. Whoever ruled the nation, Tory squires ruled the countryside and clung on as late or later than 1945. The patrician voice of the great Whig aristocrats faded earlier, though it went on speaking in the voice of its last great representative, Bertrand Russell, who died only in 1970.

Few societies have succeeded as well as England in suppressing disorder, especially after an upheaval as divisive as the Civil War. J. H. Plumb in *The Growth of Political Stability in England* was right to emphasise the trend of his title, although given the romanticising of revolution during the 1960s, a study of stability was not in the fashion. Anthony Wagner makes a good case in *Pedigree and Progress* that theories which downplay social stability are based on an imperfect understanding of genealogy and of the prolonged influence of certain families, although analysis based on a mastery of detail like his likewise remains out of fashion.

At the national level, intra-elite conflict was contained but squabbles over property among individual proprietors still surfaced, notably over shares of the common land which had been enclosed and carved up. The Veblenesque leisure class comprised of landowners was happy to acquire more resources via the large rent-seeking element in the enclosure movement. That great land grab was as much a seeking of market share as an encouragement to economic growth. H. J. Habakkuk thought that in order to become landowners, purchasers were willing to accept one or one-and-a-half per cent per annum less on their money than they might have been able to earn by other investments. Evidence of great but unproductive investment is evident, to repeat the point, in monumental country houses, long park walls, big kennels and even bigger stables, all of which are easy to observe.

Aristocrats were the ones who embellished their estates most lavishly. They spent fortunes on Grand Tours and built houses stuffed with the furnishings, paintings and statuary they brought back. They landscaped their parks, whatever the disruption to the locality. The rural rich thus formed what might be called a 'consumption elite' inclined to prefer social display over productive assets, except in some measure for farming or occasionally (where estates offered special opportunities) mining or canal building. More than one author also labels them, together with the gentry, as an 'alien elite', marrying their own kind and mixing with local populations only *de haut en bas*. By the end of the seventeenth century the Eton community was already large enough to form its own marriage market, just as in modern times (according to the *Economist*) Wykehamists who get divorced commonly cite other Wykehamists as the co-respondents.

As a multitude of biographies reveal, aristocrats and to a lesser extent the gentry were exempt from common sanctions and, despite the mannered nature of their society, even from the requirements of common decency. A nightly procession of four footmen with a stretcher removed the bibulous eleventh Duke of Norfolk from his dining table. That there was one law for the rich and another for the poor was seldom challenged and rarely successfully. In Gloucestershire, Edmund Chamberlayne received no punishment for shooting one of his tenants whose wife he had seduced. A marked feature was the way the rich acquired a protective belt of sycophantic professionals, like lawyers and land agents who identified with the interests of their employers. Nor have biographers of the great landowners always distanced themselves from sycophancy.

Obviously not every proprietor was a wastrel and some of them sponsored learned men who made signal discoveries, for instance the Lansdownes of Bowood, Calne, supported both Joseph Priestley, discoverer of oxygen, and Jan Ingenhousz, discoverer of photosynthesis. Occasional landowners made scientific advances themselves. In the same corner of Wiltshire, Henry Fox-Talbot invented photography (ironically from frustration that his daughters could draw and he could not). But the number of actual achievements on this scale was disproportionately tiny, just as Gilbert

White, the 'father of natural history', cannot by himself redeem the Church of England's boast that it put an educated man in every parish. The incentives for productive research were just too few.

Historians often concentrate on change but those who have looked closely at rural life since the Restoration (indeed before it) end by emphasising continuity, although in practice this means slow change within a remarkably static framework. Village life in the days of the common fields was strictly self-regulating, subject only to ratification by the manorial courts. Many of the features persisted intact for prolonged periods and some communal institutions for allocating resources are only now at their very last gasp. At the same time, paradoxically, innovations in farming and manufacturing were absorbed. New crops combined in fresh rotations permitted a shift from growing grain in the clay vales to ploughing up the grass of the light-soiled uplands. Seemingly the innovations economised on labour. Certainly labour did leave the land and move by stages London-wards and later northwards, according to the evidence of the Settlement Certificates whereby a parish acknowledged responsibility for taking back the holders should they threaten to become charges on the poor rates. This gave rise to despatching people back to their places of origin, especially pregnant women whose offspring would otherwise acquire a right of residence where they happened to be born. These cruel instances do not negate the fact that plenty of labour quit the countryside for London and other towns and later for the colonies. Between 1750 and 1914 the problem was simply that not enough people did so to bring about a very significant rise in the wages of those who stayed behind.

Poverty had been a problem for centuries but was exacerbated by a reduction in the number of small farms whose occupants had hitherto been independent. Technical changes in husbandry reshaped land use, though there was some inertia because leases typically stipulated that tenants must continue to farm according to the custom of the county, besides refraining from ploughing up permanent pasture and agreeing to plant hedgerow trees (thus providing fixed capital that would normally have been the landlord's responsibility). These clauses imposed some inflexibility on practice, which once more shows that institutions were not finely attuned to emerging opportunities. Against the restrictive covenants in leases were ranged the permeation of introduced crops, the imperatives of the market and the eventual imposition of enclosure, all creating tensions between old and new.

Hundreds of reminiscences of life among the rural working class in the nineteenth and twentieth centuries have now been published. Many are eloquent and thousands of colourful anecdotes have survived from those bleak times. One outstanding and sharply observed contribution is *Salt of the Earth: The Life and Work of Bygone Farm Labourers* by D. A. Trigg. Another is *The Jubilee Boy* by George Swinford, born 1887, who lived to be 100 in Filkins, Oxfordshire. Protein was scarce and Mr Swinford reports that his mother once baked a pie full of ninety-one house sparrows that he and his brothers had caught. Individual circumstances varied from region to region, according to period, local ecology, farming system, land use and whether a village was 'open' and therefore available for incomers to settle or 'closed' under a squire's thumb. How, then, can individual or local testimony be seen to be representative? At the statistical level it cannot but the sheer volume of evidence repeated and repeated from place to place should be sufficient to overwhelm scepticism. The convergent observations of so many eyewitnesses must be believed. They provide more insight than generalised tables of wage-rates, which are often based on sweeping assumptions or interpolated and extrapolated from fragments. The innumerable first-hand sources that survive are often fungible, the examples cited in one case standing in for others.

Landed proprietors were adept at passing the burdens and risks of husbandry onto their tenants and in turn tenant farmers were able to pass costs onto the labourers (e.g. standing them off when the weather was bad). Ancient practices persisted longest in the most remote districts. In Victorian times, farm families on the Cotswolds were much intermarried and according to an author who was one of them, the Garnes, were highly insular and even damagingly inbred. The backwoods attitudes of farmers in North Devon as late as the Second World War have to be read to be believed, for example in Nancy Phelan's *The Swift Foot of Time*.

Repression of the poor became intense in the nineteenth century and not merely because of the Game Laws. In 1834 a labourer at Winstone, Gloucestershire, broke one panel of a looking glass in a house of which the Rev. Sir Windsor Baynton Sandys was the tenant, apparently by accident, but two days later was fined the large sum of £4.10s. plus 10s. costs to Sandys, with the alternative of two months' hard labour. The extent of callousness may be judged from the fact that two years later at Southrop in the same county a blacksmith got seven weeks in gaol, three of them in solitary confinement, for stealing 40 lb. of coal; he had 'spots of lepisosy' (sic) all over his body. Another labourer got two months' hard labour for stealing two ducks; he had 'marks of scarvy' (sic) on his face. Wherever one looks in eighteenth- and nineteenth-century England there was meanness. Twigs and wood chips were sold to poor people desperate for fuel and the butler at Breamore House, Hampshire, dried out the tea leaves to sell to them. Northamptonshire chapels are built of red brick because the squires denied their builders use of the pits where stone could be dug.

Rather than relieve the ills of the time, deference was preserved at all costs and was taken to be part of the natural order. A history of Thruxton, near Andover, Hampshire, published in 1981 records that within living memory village women curtseyed to the lady of the manor. First-hand testimony about labour's plight at earlier periods is understandably rare, eloquent exceptions being letters lauding South Australia from Jacob Baker, originally from Hodson, near Swindon. He had been refused an opportunity to speak at a farmers' meeting in 1850 and had emigrated, but English and Scottish newspapers published his letters. Ordinarily villagers had no effective or recognised political 'voice'. Farm workers rose in 1830 and combined in Arch's union in the 1870s but met implacable resistance on both occasions. The religious equivalent of political opposition was nonconformity but this, which had been the province of professional men in late seventeenth century, was stilled in the next century, when the chapels were abandoned to poorer classes. Lack of 'voice' left only 'exit'—an option taken by the more energetic, who removed themselves to the cities or overseas. The process is not easy to observe in the histories of individual places and is best pieced together from an amalgamation of sources. Those who left largely vanish and, although letters from some who went to the colonies do survive, few have been published.

Where there was charity it stigmatised its recipients. At Tetbury, Gloucestershire, allocations of common land were denied to anyone who had been on poor relief—the very people who might have benefited most from a share of what was, after all, one of their own assets. The charity board in the church at Swinbrook, Oxfordshire, lists a bequest of green coats for the poor and also notes something which is not unusual, that other bequests had been 'lost', meaning misappropriated. Southern England was a top-down society and it may be noted that when additional gardens were provided they were *allotments* rented out by the squires. They were allotted rather than communally instigated and were not people's gardens like the Volkstuin in Holland.

In the early nineteenth century observers lamented that once-spruce cottage homes had turned slovenly. Goods were scarce as early indoor photographs show. The poor kept away from church services at Aldbourne, Wiltshire, in the early nineteenth century because they had no decent clothes to wear and more widely it is said that it was mainly the better-off who attended communion services. The habit of servant girls trying to dress like their betters, meaning in some semblance of the fashion, irritated their employers for centuries. Like the gripe by farmers that each generation of labourers was more work-shy than its fathers, the cavilling appears time and again. In her *Description of Malvern* of 1822, Mary Southall writes of Lady Lytellton: 'observing that at present, the peasantry of Great Malvern, are so earnestly desirous of obtaining light and genteel work, that farmers find it difficult to procure weeders; and aware of the baneful effects arising from an improper love of dress among female servants, she has endeavoured to check the growing evil'. The outcome was a 'School of Ancient Industry, for Spinning of Wool, Flax, Hemp, Knitting, &c. &c. erected on Malvern Chase through the liberality of Lady Lytellton, Edward Foley, Esq., of Stoke Edith Park, Earl Beauchamp, and others'. An 'unadorned' building was erected and reading and religious duties taught. Likewise the vicar of Malvern planned a 'Female Servants' Benefit Institution' with the aim of inducing them 'to dress in a manner becoming their humble stations in life'. These initiatives might be thought of as private enterprise sumptuary legislation.

Poverty, disdain and humiliation persisted much later, if not always to that degree. Farmers may have found it hard to hire weeders yet male unemployment seemed intractable during depressions like those of the 1820s, 1890s and 1930s. Even with Lloyd George's five shillings per week pension, the old found it hard to manage and Mollie Harris says that the wraithlike old women at the cottage doors in the Oxfordshire village where she grew up in the 1920s were in reality half-starved. Little was wasted in such societies. No sources of protein or firing were neglected, however humble and of whatever low quality they might be. Every biological item was put to use. Gorse was cropped short to use in bakers' ovens or cottage grates. Where the right of turbary existed, turf was dug for the fire, as in rural Ireland. Cow dung was sometimes collected for fuel and in places was dried on an industrial scale to be sold for the purpose. Parish ovens economised on fuel by sharing the heat; the alternative of cooking at home involved throwing all the ingredients together in one big pot, again to save on fuel. Coln St Aldwyn, a village next to two great Gloucestershire estates, had a public bath house heated from the bakery: in the 1950s a bath cost four pence. Most villages, of course, had no bath house nor did cottages have bathrooms.

Housing was one of the sorest points. Considerable building in the late sixteenth and early seventeenth centuries had already failed to keep pace with demand, yeomen farmers being especially unwilling to release land for the purpose. Cheap and flimsy parish houses put up by the overseers were sometimes pulled down or burned down by the neighbours. From the end of the eighteenth century the stock of dwellings utterly failed to match the size of population. Bishopstone, South Wiltshire, appears thoroughly exceptional in that, after fifty-seven people had emigrated to Australia in 1838, houses were actually demolished. At that date there was usually a distinct shortage and dwellings were divided among occupants. They became impossibly crowded, as village histories report. On census night, 30 March 1851, twenty-seven people were sleeping in barns on the farms where they worked at Burbage, Wiltshire.

The effects of population growth may be seen in the construction of additional church seating in the form of west-end galleries in the first half of the nineteenth century and from the growing number of chapels where villagers had become disgusted with the way that clergy of the established church sided with landowners during the Last Labourers' Revolt of 1830. Towards the end of the nineteenth century, when the rural population was falling again, galleries in churches were removed and cottages were deserted. There are parishes that still contain old cottage sites identifiable by remnant garden plants or sections of box hedge. In the interwar years of the twentieth century the number of houses increased by 30 per cent whereas the population rose by only 10 per cent. Crowding may thus have been reduced but the increased number of dwellings was still not enough fully to offset rural (and urban) slum clearance or to compensate for loss of income during the slump. As the Second World War began, people could be found living in old railway carriages with no heating, sanitation or water on tap.

Contrary to the notions of institutional design and positive effects present in Ronald Coase's influential theories about how the world works, landed institutions seem inadvertent hand-me-downs (if one is comforted by touching base with great authorities, this interpretation might be seen as more akin to the equally famous viewpoint of Friedrich Hayek). They evolved to safeguard special interests that can be described only as selfish. They were products of fashionable imitation with a stress on consumption and display; they were versions of old arrangements reinforced to maintain the predominance of a narrow caste and bolster what, for its members, was a favourable distribution of income. In short, the estate system and the governments that protected it operated as a giant rent-seeking machine. Admittedly the wealth created in the eighteenth and nineteenth centuries was so great that a separate stratum of bourgeoisie appeared in the towns alongside the increasing number of landowners in the countryside. Yet, although not every new fortune was deposited in the soil, a high proportion was moved there, virtually immobilising a vast share of capital in dubious agricultural arrangements.

Economic growth, once in train, was bound to challenge the existing holders of wealth and power. All they could do was delay or adapt to it, and a few entrepreneurial types apart, they did engage in plenty of what turned out to be delaying tactics. The shape and distributional ends of the landed system had been to the taste of the Puritan grandees of the 1650s and, being even more to Royalist taste, were ratified in 1660 and again in 1688. They lasted because they were integral to the prevailing social, political and economic constellations of power. Growth and industrialisation sprang from other roots and were not always welcomed by landowners, who preferred their environs undisturbed by commerce and liked local communities unchallenged by prosperous tradesmen. Some proprietors vigorously resisted change, such as the Duke of Rutland who prevented Richard Arkwright's Bakewell cotton mill from damaging his trout fishery or Lord Digby who starved Willmott's water-powered silk mills at Sherborne, Dorset, because Lady Digby preferred the sight of a full pond. Occasional landowners who happened to find coal or iron on their property might find industry acceptable but over most of the country the landed classes looked with greater favour on tradesmen who made hand-crafted luxuries and consumption goods for nearby markets.

Notwithstanding highly successful defences of sport and amenity, economic growth and industrialisation did go ahead. Enormous riches were generated and the landed system survived because the ownership of an estate was one of the rewards. Manufacturers were, so to speak, co-opted into the prevailing archaic system. The system has always represented and continues to represent a misallocation of land, labour and capital towards uses that are either not very productive or are blatantly unproductive. Land is substantially devoted to the leisure purposes of a few, including activities that are scarcely conducive to animal welfare. Labour is hired for unnecessary outdoor work and needless domestic service. The public is denied access to much of the nation's land. Farming on the acres used to produce food is subsidised by the taxpayer. Not that this is widely understood. According to the European Commission, quoted in the *Financial*

Times (12 January, 2016), 40 per cent of the UK population have not so much as heard of the Common Agricultural Policy and the support that taxpayers thereby give to farm incomes. Any social benefits have always proved incidental whereas the malign results are glaring, especially when the peculiarly English mode of allocating and using the countryside is compared with practices elsewhere in the developed world, such as parts of Scandinavia. Viewing the past, let alone the present, with moral repugnance and documenting a litany of abuses, while justified, is not of course the end of the matter but is consistent with the suggestion that alternative arrangements might be more efficient as well as fairer.

For much of history inadequate worker housing was provided. There was not enough nutritious food or heating. Educational provision and even the teaching of basic literacy were resisted and took centuries before being established as rights; an uninformed and docile cottager class was understood as being in the interests of the well-to-do. The precise extent and even the definition of poverty, not to mention its fluctuations, may be topics of scholarly dispute but the existence of deprivation on a large scale for immensely long periods is not debatable. The worst rural poverty has been alleviated by the Welfare State but even today the bottom 20 per cent of villagers, especially those reliant on the old age pension, are only scraping by. They are not however very visible. Their presence is masked by the obvious prosperity of others.

None of this should be taken as a plea for formal equality of income or equal land ownership or as an ivory-tower dream that the country might be a better place had the ambitions of the Diggers or Levellers been attained. That solution would have eaten its children like every other revolution. The argument that equality might reduce incentives is unfortunately credible and a flat distribution of ownership is in any case politically so unlikely that the notion is hypothetical. The upheaval involved would be unendurable, for it should always be considered how policies might affect the widows and orphans. Strict equality of landownership would lead to an immiserating fragmentation of holdings and frustrate economies of scale in farming. It would clog the workings of the land market. Such 'natural' experiments as there have been, for example the textbook study of the inequality which replaced the equitable distribution of cigarettes in a prisoner-of-war camp overnight, suggest that initial equality might not last long anyhow. Yet the distribution of property in England is so skewed it might be advantageous somewhat to flatten it along Scandinavian lines. The will for this does not exist; what does exist is an inherited structure of power that would thwart it. Such is the situation. Whether a densely populated and increasingly urban society will tolerate this indefinitely is an open question.

Agriculture no longer produces much of a share of national output or of the food we eat, and employs only the tiniest fraction of the labour force. But the continued ownership of large blocks of land by a tiny proportion of the population that has not acquired it by productive effort and remains starkly segregated from its fellow citizens is fundamental to England having become one of the most unequal societies in the developed world. It is a historical anomaly. It is undesirable through continuing to decide ownership by the hereditary principle and placing control in the hands of a small group with no necessarily verifiable expertise. Farm entrants to new Dutch polders have been required to pass examinations and there is reason to think that the land of England might be better run by selecting superior and less self-absorbed people than those who own it now—and many more of them. Although it cannot be said that the estate system takes all land outside the market (since whatever the short-run 'stickiness' estates remain in principle tradeable commodities), the impression is certainly of a non-market bloc occupying an unconscionable share of landed resources. One reason may be that the very largest estates tend to remain in the hands of ancient families. For all the shocks and developments, current arrangements have been resilient over the centuries. But the longevity of an arrangement guarantees neither its economic optimality nor its social desirability.

The principle of estate ownership survived drastic political and economic upheavals, such as the Norman Conquest, the Wars of the Roses, the Civil Wars, the depressions of the late nineteenth and early twentieth centuries and two world wars. Far reaching though some of these shifts were, ultimately they did little more than replace or revive the dominant occupying personnel. Change seldom threatened, much less overturned, the organising of landholding in the form of estates: the new wine was always in much the same old bottles. More revolutionary threats, such as land nationalisation or the establishment of a free peasantry, were discussed at times but never came close to fruition.

The constituent episodes of agrarian history are well known and have often been studied by specialists. Specific periods were however so marked by particular experiences as to divert attention from the long-term unity, structural similarity and endless recurrences in rural history. The almost perpetual recruitment of outside money by the landed sector, the subsequent frivolous use of much of the countryside and the resultant congealing of rural society and economy have seldom been treated as a single story. The largest category of estates, the one that set the tone, was the most stable, because its owners were the super-rich with the largest tracts or greatest extra-agricultural resources. The occupation of lesser estates was somewhat more volatile. They had been bought because an aspiration to landownership was a magnet for entrants with what proved to be shallower pockets, not infrequently military men, who were more readily dislodged by economic downturns. The prevalence and longevity of the estate system as a whole disguises the fate of these individuals. From the point of view of very long-run landownership they were perhaps little more than noise in the system.

Although some incomers may have lasted only a generation or two, they helped to perpetuate existing arrangements, with all the social, sporting and snobbish implications that so fascinate English (and foreign) tourists and titillate the audience for romantic works about country house life. 'The English country house casts a long, rose-tinted shadow', states a review in the *Economist* (7 May 2016) about a book on the subject. The same piece observes, with no discernible trace of irony, that life was tough for owners and their families. Totally ignoring the squalor and toil below stairs, it laments that 'women, in particular, were confronted with gruelling social expectations: a seven-day shooting party, for example, would require multiple outfits for every day of the week, and spending whole seasons like this was arduous'.

Economists, if they are not scrupulous, can wash out social attitudes and whole sequences of events. Aggregative studies tend to have this weakness. Colin Clark claimed in *The Economics of 1960* (written in 1942) that 'political and social upheavals, however violent, have surprisingly little effect on the long-term trend of economic events'. He measured this by proportionate changes in real income (aggregate output) per occupied person, adjusted for changes in working hours. By this means Clark succeeded in dampening such minor fluctuations as the First World War and the interwar depression. He sidelined unemployed resources, such as the 22 per cent of the workforce out of work in 1932. Although up to a point he was correct that upheavals have had less impact than customarily expected, we should not follow his example of trivialising the past by demoting its upheavals. Enough historical disturbances have been described here to refute the charge. Yet the guiding structures of English rural society did persist through all its ups and downs, with their form strikingly inviolate and their operation soon restored after even that great-est of shocks, the Civil War. Landownership has been perpetually resup-plied as an epiphenomenon of the wealth of an industrial nation that began as almost exclusively agrarian. Less unequal arrangements might have per-mitted more bottom-up entrepreneurship in agriculture, more social mobility and more democracy. These tendencies were stifled century after century by the hierarchy of class, the restricted expression of political choice and sport's interference with farming. They reveal the estate system as social and market failure on a grand and enduring scale.

Sources and Further Reading

Agricultural Economics Research Institute. (1944). *Country planning.* Oxford: Oxford University Press.

Allen, D. W. (2009). A theory of the pre-modern British aristocracy. *Explorations in Economic History, 46,* 299–313.

Allen, D. W. (2011). *The institutional revolution.* Chicago: University of Chicago Press.

Barrett, H. (2000). *A good living.* Ipswich: Old Pond.

Barrett, H. (2001). *Early to rise; A Suffolk morning.* Ipswich: Old Pond.

Bell, A. (1936). *Corduroy.* London: John Lane The Bodley Head.

Bence-Jones, M. (1965–72). The origins of the English landed gentry. In *Burke's peerage & gentry* (18th ed., Vol. 3). Bury St Edmund's: Burke's Peerage Ltd.

Burritt, E. (1868). *A walk from London to land's end and back.* London: Sampson Low.

Clark, C. (1942). *The economics of 1960.* London: Macmillan.

Fortey, R. (2017). *The wood for the trees.* London: William Collins.

Geddes, A. (n.d.). *Samuel Best and the Hampshire labourer.* Andover: Local History Society.

Green, J. (2008). *Changing scenes: Celebrating 150 years of the Tenbury Agricultural Society 1858–2008.* Tenbury Wells: Tenbury Agricultural Society.

Hobson, D. (1999). *The national wealth.* London: HarperCollins.

Horn, P. (1992). *High society: The English social elite, 1880–1914.* Stroud: Alan Sutton.

Horn, P. (2015). *Country House Society: The private lives of England's upper class after the First World War.* Stroud: Amberley.

Hudson, W. H. (1928). *Hampshire days.* London: Duckworth.

Hughes, T. (1906). *Tom Brown's schooldays.* London: J M Dent & Sons.

Jones, E. (2005). The land that Richard Jefferies inherited. *Rural History, 16,* 83–93.

Jones, E. L. (2010). *Locating the industrial revolution: Inducement and response.* Singapore: World Scientific.

Jones, E. (2016). Introduction to Richard Jefferies. In *The farmer's world.* Foulsham: Petton Books.

Keltner, D. (2016). *The power paradox: How we gain and lose influence.* London: Allen Lane.

Knowles, C. (1981). *Sparsholt and Lainston.* London: Phillimore.

Martin, E. W. (Ed.). (1967). *Country life in England.* London: Country Book Club.

Mulvagh, J. (2008). *Madresfield: The real Brideshead.* London: Doubleday.

Orr, J. (1916). *Agriculture in Oxfordshire: A survey.* Oxford: Clarendon Press.

Pinnell, B. (1987). *Country house history around Lymington, Brockenhurst and Milford-on-Sea.* Lymington: Privately printed.

Rogers, B. (2002). *The green road to nowhere: The life of an English village.* London: Aurum Press.

Torr, C. (1979). *Small talk at Wreyland.* Oxford: Oxford University Press.

Walthew, I. (2007). *A place in my country.* London: Weidenfeld & Nicolson.

Whitlock, R. (1990). *A Victorian village.* London: Robert Hale.

Williamson, H. W. (Ed.). (1946). *Richard Jefferies: Hodge and his masters.* London: Faber & Faber.

Wilmot, S. (1990). The business of improvement: Agriculture and science culture in Britain, c.1700–c.1870. *Historical Geography Research Series,* 24.

INDEX

© The Author(s) 2018
E. L. Jones, *Landed Estates and Rural Inequality in English History*,
Palgrave Studies in Economic History,
https://doi.org/10.1007/978-3-319-74869-6

Printed in the United States
By Bookmasters